Graham Wade

# The Shape
# of
# Music

*An Introduction to Form in Classical Music*

Allison & Busby
London : New York

First published 1981 by
Allison & Busby Limited
6a Noel Street, London W1V 3RB, England
and distributed in the USA by
Schocken Books Inc.
200 Madison Avenue, New York, NY 10016

**British Library Cataloguing in Publication Data:**

Wade, Graham.
  The shape of music.
  1. Music
  I. Title
  780 ML160
  ISBN 0-85031-427-5
  ISBN 0-85031-428-3 Pbk


Set in 10/12 point Times by Alan Sutton Publishing Ltd.
Printed and bound by Camelot Press, Southampton

# Contents

# for Beth

# Acknowledgements

The author would like to express his deep appreciation for all those who provided encouragement in the writing of this book; in particular, thanks are due to Bill Swainson, from whom the idea originally came, and to Nicholas Reed, Librarian at the City of Leeds College of Music, whose generous cooperation was invaluable. The efforts of my wife, Elizabeth, in checking and typing the final manuscript were magnificent beyond description; without her wisdom and endurance this book would never have seen the light of day.

**Also by**
**Graham Wade**

*Guitar Method Volumes I & II* (with recorded cassettes),
(International Correspondence Schools, London)
*Traditions of the Classical Guitar*
*Your Book of the Guitar*

# Preface

Although Graham Wade's new book is subtitled "an introduction to form in classical music", it is in fact much more. Miraculously, in my view, he has produced a work of profound erudition which at the same time is compulsive, informative reading for the non-specialist music lover.

His field of reference is wide, his style entertaining — a rare accomplishment in musicology — and both the professional musician as well as the enthusiastic, untrained concert-goer should acquire *The Shape of Music* as essential reading. I know of no book like this on the subject of music; and apart from the wealth of essential information which it contains, it is every bit as absorbing as a work of popular, general literature on any subject.

Dr Malcolm Williamson, CBE
Master of the Queen's Music

# Introduction

The shape of music, like the shape of landscape, is fundamental to its appeal. Music, like geography, has its Himalayas, its flatlands, its oceans and its backwaters. Understanding at least some of the reasons for such variety is essential if music is to be fully appreciated.

Unfortunately many books about music are enormously complicated. They expect us to have considerable experience of listening to many types of music. This book is not entirely simple. To write about music is to deal with a whole range of complicated material. But I have tried, here, not to take too much for granted and to build up step by step the outlines of European musical forms and developments.

The book begins by considering the significance of the composer, that elusive figure who gives us music worth listening to. Composers exist rather like fish in the sea, apparently free to swim in any direction yet actually pulled this way and that by many strong currents and tides. The shape of music grows from both personal choice and historical influence. To understand something of each aspect is a vital part of listening to music.

At the end of certain chapters there is a list of various relevant compositions. Some of these guides to further listening are quite long and no reader is expected to sit down for a marathon hearing of all the items selected. The aim has been to choose compositions which illustrate the points made in each chapter and to offer the reader the widest possible choice. All of the works listed are easily available on record and cassette and many of them are frequently included in concerts and broadcasts.

The shape of music constantly changes. One fashion yields to another, certain instruments become obsolete and retreat into silence, new structures and new sounds constantly emerge. It can all be rather confusing. Yet the adventure of music, past and present, is there for us to explore and enjoy, a life-long journey of discovery.

GRAHAM WADE
May, 1981

# 1

# The Composer

All music has to begin somewhere and it originates, one way or another, with a "composer". A composer is a craftsman, a maker, a builder, also a designer, bringing into the world something which did not previously exist and which may prove of great value to humanity. A furniture-maker uses wood to build his creations and an architect moulds concrete, stone, steel and other materials into useful, habitable structures. The composer works with the invisible but powerful properties of sound, filling the world with patterns, vibrations and musical shapes.

The composer feels a need to create music, often being driven by an inner compulsion from an early age to attempt the creation of music. But, as well as creating music and performing on various instruments, composers must also listen to the music going on around them, observing and absorbing techniques and styles.

Every nation, race, tribe, creed and social background produces people skilled in the art of music. In primitive societies music plays a particularly vital part in daily life. In this context music is rarely written down formally, but musical secrets are passed from one generation to another orally. Improvisation is vital here and the roles of composer and player are virtually one and the same.

However, improvisation is rarely a matter of playing whatever comes into one's head. It usually involves a rather complicated set of guidelines within which the music functions. The player/composer must first master these rules before being in a position to advance the art according to his or her own personal insights.

Indian music with its intricate ragas, Andalucian flamenco with numerous forms and variations, and most styles of jazz improvisation with fixed chord sequences derived from melodies, are examples of disciplined, informed improvisation. Many varieties of African, Arabic and Oriental folk music also operate along similar lines. Composers in these cultures submit themselves to a rigid discipline in order to master playing and compositional techniques. Such apprenticeships are often lifelong as well as being extremely demanding, both physically and mentally.

In European music over the last five centuries improvisation for soloists and groups has frequently been a necessary part of a musician's life. But the art of composing became more and more closely linked with writing music down using a device now called musical notation. Notation enables composers to reach a wide international public of players and listeners, and to pass on to later generations the essence of their musical ideas.

One practical result of notation is to burden the composer with a great task. Literally millions of notes have to be put down on paper. Unlike the contemporary novelist, for example, who can use a typewriter, a composer has no such mechanical means to lighten the labour. A piece of music of five minutes playing time, composed for a large orchestra, might take the composer hundreds of hours to write down.

As well as writing the notes down, the composer must add suitable expression marks conveying many subtle distinctions of meaning. The preparation of orchestral parts is also a massive labour. The composer must not only be an imaginative musician, but also a patient worker, willing to put up with long periods of comparative drudgery in order to achieve something of value. It cannot be wondered at if some composers in history seem to have pursued a rather isolated existence as they struggled with their sonatas, symphonies, concertos and operas, slowly shaping them in their heads and on paper. Some composers have worked with lightning speed, but others agonize over their manuscripts with the slow deliberation of tortoises.

As far as the listener is concerned all composers from all cultures deal with the same basic materials. They create melodies and provide accompaniments, they set our feet tapping or our heads swaying with rhythmic patterns, they borrow or imitate sounds from the world of nature and humanity.

Great melodies come from the properties of the human voice and almost all musical instruments relate to the voice. The most exciting rhythms are taken in the first instance from the universal beating of heart and pulse, and from the complex varied activities of the body in dancing, movement and gesture. Natural sounds such as the sea, trees, streams, birdsong, galloping horses and thunderstorms can provide inspiration for composers. But so also can the noises of human activity such as the movements of men pulling on ropes at sea, the clatter of the spinning wheel, the rhythms of machines, the blacksmith's hammer or the marching of armies.

Just as the painter makes us more aware of colour, form and movement in the visual world, so the composer has the capacity to make us more sensitive to the world of hearing. The story of music tells how musicians strive constantly to make patterns of sound more meaningful and more immediate to themselves and to their listeners.

# 2

# Sound

Sound is vibration. From birth onwards we are absorbed, soothed, frightened, or indifferent to, millions of varieties of vibration. It just happens that we have been born into the noisiest century ever known, a fact we all must come to terms with. In the skies above our heads, in the streets, in the factory, even in the office, noise, noise, and more noise. Aircraft, pneumatic drills, cars and lorries, bulldozers, factory machines, trains . . .

The music of the twentieth century has to take full account of the times we live in. Modern music certainly reflects the turmoil and cacophony of daily living. Moreover contemporary composers have been keen to develop novel techniques for creating a wide variety of sound effects. Electronic music, ingenious uses of amplification, and numerous evolving species of electric instruments (including keyboard, basses and violins, as well as guitars) have changed the textures of musical sound.

It is not surprising if new instruments are invented for composers to exploit. Musical tastes are in a perpetual state of change throughout all historical eras. The actual make-up of ensembles and orchestras from the Middle Ages onwards never remains static or rigidly fixed.

Unfamiliar instruments have always been welcomed by composers and new combinations of existing and accepted instruments are a common feature of the development of orchestral and group music. In previous centuries composers sometimes became preoccupied with such oddities as the glass harmonica or the arpeggione, or hybrids such as the lute-harpsichord (a device played like a keyboard but sounding like a lute). Nowadays composers experiment similarly with electronic feedback, multiple tape-recorders and many kinds of synthesizer.

Musical development is fortunately stabilized by various factors. For one thing the human ear predetermines the range and intensity of sound available to the composer. Sounds which are too high-pitched or too low-pitched (such as the notes at the extreme ends of a pianoforte) are not really convenient for sustained composition being both monotonous and indistinguishable from each other to the average human ear. Similarly sounds which are too soft or too loud are not acceptable over too long a listening period, though they may be tolerable for a little while. Prolonged exposure to sounds of great volume can of course damage the sensitive mechanism of the ear.

Another constant factor in the process of composition is the capability of the human voice. Music tends to be written for the more comfortable ranges of the various types of voice, generally avoiding too much concentration on extremes of sound at either end of "high" and "low". In this instance too many low notes and too many high notes are not only potentially tedious for the listener but can also strain the singer's voice. The composer has to learn to respect the possibilities and limitations of the human vocal cords.

Each kind of voice, ranging from the deep bass to the high soprano, possesses its own characteristic sound qualities. By mixing together several types of voice within a choir composers through the ages have succeeded in creating amazingly varied patterns of vocal music. From the skilful combination of distinctive voices emerged those contrasting lines of sound known as "counterpoint" and from this, after a due process of historical development, came the complexities of harmony.

The human voice was, after all, the original musical instrument and it remains the most evocative and compelling of all.

# The Musical Scale

Anyone who has learned a musical instrument knows that those who wish to become expert performers have to spend quite a lot of time practising scales. Most professional musicians keep their playing muscles supple by daily exercises of this kind whilst singers find scales invaluable in developing the full range of the voice.

All this hard work is inspired by the knowledge that melody, harmony and musical theory are firmly based on the patterns of tones and half tones which form the basis of European scales. The actual notes of the scales give us the raw materials of music from which composers can build their works.

The European scales took hundreds of years to develop to the system we are familiar with today. Other musical cultures, such as those of India, Arabia and the Far East, evolved totally different scale formations.

The word **scale** is derived from the Latin word *scala*, meaning a "ladder". By means of this ladder music ascends or descends by a convenient sequence of rungs. In the western scales each ladder is made up of eight principal steps. Each step is given a letter name, and the scale is named according to the letter it starts on.

Here are the eight steps of the scale of C (the Italian names for the notes also being included):

```
                                              C
                                      B       do
                                      si
                              A
                      G       la
              F       sol
      E       fa
  D   mi
C do  re
do
```

As the scale is made up of eight notes, the distance or interval between the two C's is known as an **octave**, from the Latin word for "eight". The interval of the octave, the essential boundary of all scales, is used by musicians the world over whatever their cultural environment. Stringed instruments, particularly those such as the violin, guitar, sitar, Arabian lute, etc. in which the player's left hand shortens the vibrating string length by pressing the string down onto the neck of the instrument, are all able to demonstrate that fact of physics which creates the octave.

If, for example, a violinist or guitarist, presses a string with the left hand onto the neck of the instrument at exactly the half-way mark between the two fixed points of the vibrating string, the player produces a note an octave higher than the open string itself. If the string is tuned to vibrate at a frequency of 440 times per second (which produces the note A), the octave note would vibrate at precisely double the frequency of the open string, i.e. at 880 vibrations per second. This simple fact of physics, that a vibrating string if divided into two equal parts will sound the same note an octave higher is the starting point for the construction of the scale.

Though all musical cultures throughout the world acknowledge the interval of the octave, few of them have come to the same conclusions on how the octave should be divided. If you examine a modern pianoforte keyboard you can see how after centuries of theoretical discussion, the European ear decided to divide the octave. Each octave is divided into twelve equal parts, called **half tones** or **semitones**. By combining half tones and tones (a tone being two semitones) in a specific order of eight steps, the western major and minor scales are built up.

The west may have settled down to dividing the octave into twelve semitones, but it is possible for the human ear to distinguish not only semitones but also those notes which can exist in between the semitones, sometimes entitled **microtones**. In the musical traditions of other cultures the octave is indeed divided into these microtones. Thus the structure and shape of such scales sound very different from those favoured by European composers.

In Indian music, as in the western scale, the seven main notes plus one to make up the octave are used, but the octave itself is divided into no fewer than twenty-two *shrutis*. These are like the western sharps and flats, though in this case being considered as not only sharp and flat but as "extremely flat" and "extremely sharp".

Arabic music is founded on a series of modes (to be dealt with in the next chapter), and again the octave is subdivided far more than in western music. The theory on which Arabic music is based goes back to the early Middle Ages.

From the characteristic patterns of scales within each musical culture, the nature of its melody is derived. Many varieties of scales have evolved through the centuries. Each part of the world grows accustomed to the specialities of its own scales, and also to its own rhythms and instrumental textures.

To the western ear the shifting tones and microtones of Indian, Arabic and Oriental music may sound rather odd, if not totally incomprehensible. Listening to music from a foreign culture is like watching baseball or cricket and not knowing the rules. However, in recent years people have been more exposed to the music of other nations and this has resulted in a wider appreciation of the common ground between musical cultures as well as in a useful understanding of essential differences.

# 4

# Tonality

All of us at some time or other have heard the chanting of monks, even if only as part of a film or television documentary. Monastic chanting is a very distinctive type of singing and its origins go far back into early Christian history.

Such music is called **plainsong** (or *cantus planus* in Latin) and became formally established as appropriate music for divine worship by Pope Gregory at the end of the sixth century. The music is also known as **Gregorian Chant** in his honour. This style was found to be very suitable for the communal singing of psalms and prayers. It was easy to sing and did not need a high level of musical training. Moreover the medieval authorities were anxious that music should not be too exciting or sensuous in divine service, and for this reason choral singing in parts and instrumental accompaniments were not allowed. The music was kept as simple as possible in contrast to the vivid splendour of much sacred music of later centuries.

Gregorian chant achieves its particular sound and mood from the kind of scales the monks used. These scales, known as **modes** were the direct ancestors of our modern western scales, both major and minor. Music as we know it today is overwhelmingly indebted to those hundreds of years of tradition when the modes dominated musical composition.

The theory governing the construction of the modes once again concerns the division of the octave into suitably spaced tones and semitones. For all practical purposes eight modes were used, each mode containing its own characteristic qualities.

If we pick out a tune on a modern piano and use just the white notes, and none of the black notes, the music will sound modal. Each of the modes was eventually given a Greek name in order to distinguish it from the others. The **Aeolian mode** can be played on a piano by using the following notes:

                                              A
                                      G
                              F
                      E
                  D
              C
          B
A

This mode closely resembles the modern harmonic minor scale of A minor:

                                              A
                                      G sharp
                              F
                      E
                  D
              C
          B
A

In the sixteenth century composers began to prefer the note G sharp to G when they wrote compositions based on the Aeolian mode. One reason for this may have been that to move from G sharp to A emphasizes the principal note of the scale more definitely and unmistakably. Thus, in this instance, a mode was slightly altered by the composers with the result that the new emerging scale was ultimately preferred and the old Aeolian mode became obsolete and dropped out of use.

In the case of the **Ionian mode** no such change was apparently necessary. This follows the pattern of a modern major scale, the scale of C:

  C

                                              B

                                    A

                              G

                        F

                  E

            D

C

In the Ionian or C major scale the principal note of C seems to
be emphasized sufficiently and composers were content to use
this scale formation more and more.

The modes influenced the composition of music from about 400
AD to the beginning of the seventeenth century. But composers
became increasingly attracted to the idea of **tonality**, and the use
of tonality meant the ultimate displacement of modal music. The
modes themselves in either plainsong or instrumental compositions have the effect of weakening and diluting tonality. This
means that each note of the modal scale is very much an equal
partner. In a truly modal work you could end on any note and it
would sound like a reasonably final and complete ending. But the
modern western scales of major and minor can only finish on the
principal note of the scale, known as the **tonic** or **keynote**, i.e.
that note on which the scale starts, opening the door of the scale
and closing it firmly at the end of the composition. Tonality
implies music which contains a particular significant "tone" or
note, to which the music consistently relates.

Surprisingly, perhaps, tonality is not easily defined, but funda-
mentally it means that a composer refers constantly to the tonic
or keynote. The properties associated with that key or scale are
assumed to be the central point, the home ground of the composition. It is possible to move away from the home ground, of
course, and sometimes quite a long way, but sooner or later the
central point will be returned to.

Steadily, the major and minor scales invaded the vocabulary of
composers. For over three hundred years from 1600, music in
Europe is really about tonality, the sense of relationships
between sounds. Even in the twentieth century, when so many
composers write music which is **atonal** (without a key), the

majority of popular music is still deeply rooted in tonality. Everyday music such as pop songs, national anthems and hymns, all conclude decisively in the home key.

The complexities of tonality are considerable. Looked at on paper the possibilities exploited by great composers are endless, yet, when the music in question is listened to, a supreme naturalness dominates the proceedings. More often than not the semimiraculous jugglings of harmony, key, melodic movement, etc., as the composer shifts his music from the home ground to new country and back again, are accepted by the listener with satisfaction and pleasure. The effect is that desired by all art, of variety within unity.

Tonality begins (and ends) with a consideration of the scale. As we have seen, each scale consists of eight notes including our precious octave. The notes of the scale all possess power, just like the pieces on a chess board. And just as in chess where pawns can sometimes win the game, the apparently less important notes of the scale can on occasion be very powerful indeed.

In order of significance for general purposes, the first note of the scale, the tonic or keynote, is the king of the scale. Everything in tonality relates to the tonic in one way or another. There may even be a particular power in a composition if a composer chooses to write a piece of music in a certain key.

The second most powerful note in the scale is the fifth note from the tonic, called the **dominant**. A chord founded on this note, or even the note itself, can often in no ambiguous manner, herald the immediate return of king tonic. The fourth note of the scale, the **subdominant**, also possesses some of this power returning us, as it were, to an awareness of the tonic.

The seventh note of the scale is called the **leading note**, leading us up to the tonic itself. The third note of the scale, aptly called the **mediant** (as it is halfway between the tonic and the dominant) has a special importance, for this note can tell us if the key is major or minor.

The second note is entitled the **supertonic**, being one above the tonic, and the sixth note is the **submediant**, being halfway between tonic and subdominant when the scale descends.

Here then is our scale set out ready for battle:

VIII Tonic

VII Leading note

VI Submediant

V Dominant

IV Subdominant

III Mediant

II Supertonic

I Tonic

Tonality definitely does not mean that a piece of music is just in one key throughout. The composer has an option which is to **modulate** into other keys. Far from weakening the home ground, modulation may well reinforce the tonality, just as absence from home in foreign lands may instil a longing for one's native country.

Moreover each major key possesses a **relative minor**, just as conversely each minor key has a **relative major**. This family relationship between major and minor is an invaluable aid to a composer who wishes temporarily to change the mood of a particular piece without departing too far distant from the home key.

The mechanisms of modulation are in themselves quite complicated, but to the listener a satisfactory modulation can be a sudden sparkle of sun on a grey sea or a vision of a new world. In the hands of a master, modulation can be so subtle that one hardly realizes it is happening. Controlling a smooth transition from one key to another (and back again) is a necessary skill for the composer and corresponds to the expertise of a racing driver in changing gears around the circuit.

The use of tonality has frequently been compared to an artist's use of colour in a painting. Many pictures are made up from one overall colour scheme, with a few tints dominating the entire canvas. In such a design blue might have a closer relationship to green and yellow than it would to, say, bright red. To the sensitive ear musical keys interact one against another just as colours juxtaposed on a canvas can affect the discerning eye. The subtle mixture of musical light and shade through tonality is not only a fascinating study, it is also the cornerstone of western music. Without at least a reasonable awareness of its implications and effects, the work of most composers is robbed of meaning.

# Melody, Counterpoint and Harmony

The history of music, as one might expect, is about increasing levels of complexity. Choirs and orchestras get bigger, more and more types of instruments are invented and used, musical works in themselves become longer and more substantial, the art of musical notation becomes ever more intricate, and the performance of music on public occasions (such as concerts or operas) grows more expensive and more elaborate. Gregorian chant could be performed by a few monks; an opera nowadays requires dozens of singers and musicians, many stage-hands and a huge theatre to achieve its effect. Yet all this development is rooted in the very nature of music itself. From the acorn of melody grows the mighty tradition of counterpoint and harmony, the musical oak tree which spans centuries.

The simplest musical texture (apart from just banging a drum or playing a single note on an instrument) is surely that of a solo voice singing a straightforward tune. To some extent the discovery of the voice's ability to pitch notes in a satisfying sequence is presumably how music began. Not many notes are needed to construct a little melody. Some primitive cultures use only three or four notes in a song, these being subjected to both repetition (with its curiously hypnotic effect) and rhythmic variation. This leads to the performance of the same notes on a musical instrument such as bamboo pipes or a stringed gourd. Another sound is thus added to the musical vocabulary of the tribe. The tune itself can be accompanied by percussion to give a little density to the sound.

It was realized fairly early on in history how the chanting of melodies could be given body and form by sheer weight of numbers. Singing in a choir was discovered to be pleasurable for the participants and moving for the listeners. Choral singing took a central place in religious, political and social occasions, as it still does. To the resonances of vocal ensemble, could then be added percussion, pipes, lyres, etc. to provide variety.

Music was used on many occasions. Religious ceremonies (including weddings and funerals), civic occasions, marching songs for armies, work songs of many kinds, festive gatherings, the sung recitation of epic tales of love, bravery and great national events — these were contexts which music could celebrate or enhance. In all such communal music the art of melody rules supreme.

Throughout the world today music still elevates melody to a supreme position. In European folk song, in Oriental, Arabic and Indian music, the voice and its melodic weavings are a most important aspect. The instruments that have evolved (apart from percussion) recreate in a subtle form, the basic patterns of sound borrowed from the singer.

Since the Middle Ages western music developed an interest in the skills of **counterpoint** and **polyphony**. Counterpoint (from a Latin term *punctus contra punctum* meaning "note against note") is first mentioned by Hucbald, a French monk, at the end of the ninth century, in a musical thesis. Since that time musicians in the west have been fascinated by what happens when against a single melody sung by one person, another melody is voiced at the same time. And why not go further and sing three, four, or half a dozen melodies simultaneously? Thus began the **contrapuntal** tradition, contrapuntal being the adjective derived from counterpoint.

Polyphony meaning "many-voiced" is the ideal word to describe the choral music of several centuries. Each section of the choir pursues an independent line of melody, yet however many parts are included, each fits into the grand design with the neat precision of a Swiss clock. (The same principles of composition then became characteristic of instrumental music as well.)

Polyphony still flourishes in the realm of ecclesiastical music. The great cathedrals of the world and their choirs continue the tradition of previous ages and the masterpieces brought into being by the geniuses of counterpoint, such as Palestrina and J.S. Bach, enthral modern music-lovers.

Developing from counterpoint came a new interest in the mysteries of **harmony**. Composers became more and more intrigued by the chemistry of sound, by what happens when one musical ingredient is added to another. During the seventeenth and eighteenth centuries the independent voices and instruments favoured by contrapuntal styles, tended towards a more unified method of composing music. Counterpoint and harmony became established as equal partners in the study of music. Previously the art of music had consisted primarily of the subtle weaving

15

together of individual threads of sound. Now composers became absorbed in harmonic blocks of sound, thinking about music not in horizontal or linear terms, but in vertical lines of progressive chordal sequences.

The second half of the eighteenth century established beyond doubt which way western music was to go. By then contrapuntal traditions were beginning to sound a little old-fashioned, and different ideas about how music should be composed were becoming firmly rooted. It was a momentous period in the development of musical history. From then on until the twentieth century it was harmony not counterpoint which dominated the principles of western music.

# The Instruments of Music

The variety of instruments is infinite, yet the actual means by which musical instruments can be made to sound are limited to four methods: plucking or bowing a string, blowing, drumming or knocking.

Musicologists have grouped the various types of instruments into the following four families. These are:

**Idiophones:** for knocking, such as cymbals, triangle or bells, or instruments such as xylophones or glockenspiels.

**Membranophones:** the drum family, in which a membrane or skin is stretched across a resonating cavity.

**Chordophones:** all stringed instruments, whether plucked (like the harp) or bowed (like the 'cello).

**Aerophones:** for blowing, such as trumpets, clarinets, flutes, bagpipes, whistles, etc.

These four groups are useful for general reference but the excitement now begins. The sheer range and scope of different types of instrument means that each culture tends to specialize in its own characteristic sounds. Chordophones of the plucked variety, for example, will include instruments as different as the Indian sitar, the Spanish guitar, the Arabic lute and the Russian balalaika. Aerophones range from the Jewish shofar (ram's horn) to the giant Alpine horn, and include the pipes of Pan, the harmonica and the trombone.

Musical instruments are known for their power to evoke the culture of particular countries. The Japanese koto, the Appalachian banjo, the Australian Aboriginal didjeridoo and the Scottish bagpipes instantly conjure up an image of their homelands. A few notes on one of these is sufficient to create the sense of "being there". This strong identity of national music is mainly brought about by instrumental colour.

These colours can also recall bygone historical eras. The sound of lute and viols will bring to life the court of Elizabeth I or can be used effectively for staging a play by Shakespeare. Crumhorns, recorders, sackbuts and citterns in "early music" are characteristic of the Middle Ages, whilst the tinkling of the harpsichord is forever reminiscent of the Baroque style of music. Similarly the massive sounds of a huge orchestra are associated with the nineteenth-century expansion of intrumental colour across a large musical canvas.

Instrumentation is a vital quality in all music. The listener learns to distinguish between various instruments and to associate certain sounds with specific periods of musical development. Style, scope and length in musical composition are closely related to instrumental colour. A symphony written for a hundred-piece orchestra would be disappointing if it lasted for only five minutes. We expect something more substantial from such a large body of musicians. On the other hand, a suite written for harpsichord or small ensemble might be tedious if prolonged for more than about a quarter of an hour.

The umbilical relationship between the shape, form and structure of compositions and the instruments available to the composer at any given time should not be forgotten. In this instance the message is indeed the medium. Though accepted conventions may be transcended by genius at all times throughout musical history, an instrument (or a particular group of instruments) will to a large extent limit the composer's imagination in one way or another. The composer's ability to get the best out of available instrumental resources in unprecedented ways is one of the main aspects of musical development.

# Notation

It took hundreds of years for musical notation to become as reliable and satisfactory as it is today. Composers now possess an international language of music through which they are able to communicate to a wide public. Various symbols, signs and marks have been evolved to give the performer a lot of information in a remarkably short space.

Pitch, duration, and rhythm of individual notes, as well as phrasing, volume, speed, shading and other subtleties, can all be conveyed through notation. A composer has the opportunity to make clear his musical thoughts through a tried and tested method whether composing for a child learning the recorder or for a large professional orchestra.

The system of writing down music is still not considered to be absolutely perfect and composers continue to add their own modifications to the art. Some instrumental techniques and sounds (especially in contemporary music) are extremely difficult to put down on paper and in modern scores composers often add a page or two of instructions by way of a preface.

Music of the past also poses problems. Obscurities abound in manuscripts of earlier centuries. The actual signs and indications may remain the same but over the years the meaning and interpretation of these can alter, with the result that musicologists spend a great deal of time trying to establish just exactly how those early composers intended their music to sound.

The effect on western music of the gradual developments in notation has been total. As a result of being able to write down their music composers have been free to indulge their imaginations. Restrictions imposed by length, number and ability of performers, and types of instruments available can be ignored. Notation allows ambitious projects to be undertaken at the composer's leisure. Even if a composer's work is not performed in his lifetime, it can be preserved for posterity. People of later generations may ultimately recognize the merit of a composition that has long languished in neglect.

Composers such as Bach, Mozart, Beethoven, Chopin and Liszt, were considered to be among the finest virtuoso instrumentalists of their day. They wrote down their works both for personal performance and for publication and consequently their brilliant compositions still challenge the minds and abilities of the world's great players.

Beethoven, one of the outstanding pianists of his time (before deafness forced him to retire from public performance) composed his greatest works for piano, string quartet and orchestra, long after he was physically capable of hearing the notes. The existence of a valid system of writing music down enabled him to make full use of his imaginative powers as a composer. We tend to take for granted the marvellous convenience of notation, but without it, the glories of European music could never have been achieved and perpetuated.

You might argue that though notation can liberate the composer it may have the effect of shackling the poor performer, who has to submit to the composer's will as revealed on the page. The player's sole function, it seems, is to re-create notes put down by somebody else with no scope for his own individuality or creative musical gifts.

This was not always so. Between the sixteenth and nineteenth centuries, the player was expected to be able to embellish and improvise on the composer's written guidelines. In our own century composers have tried to restore some of this initiative to the player by including in the score moments of improvisation when the performer's musical contribution can be added to the composer's. This recalls an important feature of the eighteenth-century concerto, known as the **cadenza**, when a performer playing with the orchestra was expected to introduce a brief solo section into the work either actually improvised on the spot or composed by himself before the concert. In this way a balance could be achieved between the demands of the composer and the performer's personal contribution.

Composers have shown themselves aware of the problem — too strict an adherence to notation can stifle the spontaneity of the player. Jazz composers such as Duke Ellington wrote music which includes both ensemble playing from the score and sections of improvisation for soloists. Other composers have been insistent on the details of the printed page, preferring the performer to undertake the role of a go-between communicating essential messages from the composer to the audience. But the world of music is very wide and every taste is catered for within it, whether composer, player or listener.

A further point about notation is necessary. What about the people who like listening to music but who cannot read notation at all? To such a person the complex score of a symphony or opera is nothing more than a mass of squiggles on the page. Does this matter?

Fortunately not! Many music-lovers, of all types of music, would be quite lost if confronted by notation. But just as the tourists on an ocean liner need know nothing about navigation, tides, stars or compasses, to enjoy the voyage, so the enjoyment of music need not depend on the ability to read the score. The art of notation is primarily the responsibility of composers, conductors and players.

Admittedly any knowledge of music will help the listener to enjoy more fully performances of any kind whether live or recorded. But music remains a pure art, filling our ears with sound that does not have to be translated back into written symbols. Music exists only when it is heard. It is the *hearer* of music not the *reader* of music who matters.

# 8

# Musical Form

So far we have dealt with the background to a composition — its composer, tonality, texture, instrumentation and notation. These elements are fundamental and knowledge of them prepares us for listening to music. But as well as being aware of such things the person who likes music ought to know as much as possible about the subject of **form**.

Expectation of coming events plays an important part in human life. We look forward to occasions such as holidays, parties, Christmas, weddings, outings, travels, etc. When these things happen we hope they measure up to our expectations which are based on previous enjoyable occasions or on what others may have told us. We know how long each activity will take (with a little allowance either way), what should happen, what could happen and what probably ought to happen and will happen.

At a sporting event the same thing applies. If we go to a football match we expect to see a game played according to the usual rules, with the correct number of players, on the appropriate size of field. The football fan knows the rules and enjoys the match in the expectation that this is a properly constituted game. The football will range up and down the limits of the pitch, the game will last only the specified length of time, and the excitement will be of the kind one would expect from this particular sport. If the referee is attacked by the crowd, or the players fight amongst themselves, this will spoil the form and structure of the game and it will turn from one kind of entertainment into something else. All sport, from golf to motor racing, from ping-pong to tossing the caber, operates on these principles allowing for freedom and variety but within the rules of the game.

Musical form is based similarly on expectations. The *Pocket Oxford Dictionary* defines "form" as "Shape, arrangement of parts . . . arrangement and style in literary or musical composition". The composer, by writing in a particular musical form, builds up a sense of rules and guidelines. These may not be as strict as the rules of football or the laws of the land, but the composer works within certain limits, and it aids his cause if the audience is in on the game.

The composer is a person speaking through music to people. The language in which he speaks, like any language, has its rules of syntax, grammar, style and usage, as well as its framework of reference within which speaker and listener can be united. Form establishes the means of communication between composer and listener. From particular musical forms the listener expects certain things and waits to see if the composer will achieve them. If the listener does not know what to expect something may still be gathered from a composition whatever the form, but less will be received than if the listener understands the language the composer is speaking.

Take, for example, a European listener who hears Indian music for the first time. We will assume that our listener knows nothing about ragas, sitars, sarods, etc. The listener present at a performance may be excited by the colour and energy of the scene, the movements of the musicians and the unusual sounds coming from the instruments. What the person may not appreciate is 1) how each raga has its own character (and is often associated with a certain time of day), 2) the nature of the tal or rhythmic pulse, 3) the significance of the alap or prelude, 4) the jor (an improvisation introducing rhythm), or 5) the jhala (the exciting climax of the piece). Neither will the listener be competent to assess whether the performance was good or bad. Many things may have been taken in and the music may have been enjoyed, but the music of India is not random or casual: it follows strict forms and without some knowledge of these rules the essential meaning of the music will be lost.

The music of southern Spain, like Indian music, is a complex art in which many rhythms and structures distinguish one form from another. Each flamenco piece, such as soleares, alegrias, malagueñas, fandango, etc., is governed by a separate identity, and woe betide the guitarist, dancer, or singer who mixes one with another.

The Spanish word "aficionado" (also applied to those who are knowledgeable about the bullfight) is bestowed on the individual who cares about, studies and becomes involved in flamenco music; it means an "informed enthusiast". The casual listener to flamenco will believe that the music palls after a while because it all seems very similar. The aficionado knows that music is like people; viewed from a distance and seen in a crowd people all look very similar — but get nearer to each one and, hey presto, they are all individuals. Form, and an awareness of musical form, is thus a process of individualizing the shapes and possibilities of music.

A knowledge of form, whatever culture or style of music we are dealing with, builds up in the listener, therefore certain expectations. These include the following:

1) **An expectation of length**

   An opera, because of its complicated form and dramatic structure, may last up to five hours or more. A symphony may take more than an hour depending on the composer and the historical period. A popular song would not be expected to last for more than a few minutes. Duration in music is a most important aspect of its form.

2) **An expectation of style**

   This covers many qualities including whether the piece is vocal or instrumental, its sound textures (e.g. melodic, contrapuntal, dissonant, etc.), the use of particular instruments according to period and composer, the size of the piece and whether it is written for solo performer, small ensemble or large orchestra.

3) **An expectation of difficulty or simplicity**

   Some musical forms will be more demanding on the listener than others. Certain types of music will require more stamina, perseverance and tolerance. This is not necessarily to do with length. Modern music for example may leave the audience in some confusion because the music by its very novelty is likely to shock or disturb them into new attitudes. A routine rendering of Beethoven's Fifth Symphony, especially to the experienced listener, (though longer than many modern works) may prove a very easy listening experience. To a young child *any* symphony may seem intolerably difficult to absorb.

4) **Expectation of repetition**

   It is a necessary requirement of musical form that each melody or theme should be thoroughly received and assimilated by the audience before new material is brought in. The processes of repetition in some types of music such as the suite, symphony, traditional jazz, folk-songs, Scottish reels etc., create a fundamental architecture of sound to which the listener responds. The psychological implications of repetition are very profound; in many cultures the insistent repeating of short melodic or rhythmic phrases to induce a hypnotic effect on listener or performer is an essential part of musical enjoyment.

5) **Expectation of development**

Music is like a river or conversation, always moving onwards, prolonging itself in new directions. The longer the piece of music, the more we might expect radical and intriguing developments. The development can also be compared to characters in a drama whose destiny is steadily revealed to us. The destiny of melodic ideas is unveiled throughout the duration of a musical form, and the lengthier works must justify themselves by achieving a worthwhile resolution and climax to the ideas that have been put forward.

6) **Expectation of an ending**

Just as music must have a beginning, it must also have an ending. The form of music is a kind of journey — setting out, travelling, and arriving at the destination. Composers have given particular care to the shaping of the ending. One work, Schubert's "Unfinished" Symphony, has attracted attention precisely because it is one of the few compositions which has no ending as such, thus bringing in both surprise and poignancy.

These expectations of length, style, degree of difficulty or simplicity, repetition, development and ending can be acquired quite easily. Each hearing of a composition, whatever its duration or complexity or cultural background, adds to our musical experience and can prepare us for further understanding of the significance of shape in music.

# 9

# Binary and Ternary

Sometimes, for no apparent reason, a tune can get inside one's head and, like an unwelcome visitor, will not leave. A tune takes us over. Whistling, humming, and singing are the first signs of possession.

What are the qualities of this kind of tune which, like an irritating sticking plaster, cannot be shaken off? Tunes such as "Clementine," "Yankee Doodle," "Old Macdonald", "When the Saints Go Marching In" or "We Shall Overcome", are immediately identifiable and eminently singable. They are all concise, and the sentiments of the words are at one with the mood of the music. All these tunes use the device of repetition to establish firmly the lines of melody.

Such popular tunes usually consist of either two parts or three parts. These structures are known in musical language as **binary** (two part) and **ternary** (three part) form.

In many popular standards and jazz compositions of the thirties and forties, composers wrote according to a very convenient ternary arrangement. The tune itself was presented in the first eight bars; this was repeated (just in case you did not get it the first time); another eight bars, appropriately called the **middle eight** — or **bridge** then followed, presenting a different tune which complemented the main tune; the first eight bars were then played again.

The result was a structure of thirty-two bars, eight plus eight, "middle eight", and eight bars of tune again. In a fox-trot or quick-step each bar possesses four beats, so each eight bars contained no less and no more than thirty-two beats. For many years popular music followed this structure with considerable regularity, imposing uniformity and a clear expectation on player and listener alike.

In a simple tune such as "Clementine" the opening statement of melody is answered by a concluding section of the same length which grows out of and complements the original melody.

A                     In a cavern, in a canyon,
                          Excavating for a mine,

B                              Dwelt a miner, forty niner,
                                 And his daughter, Clementine.

(The sections, as we see, can be described as "A" and "B") The clarity and conciseness of this structure make a tune such as "Clementine" as durable as oak. This straightforward binary shape welds together two matching units as firmly as two halves of a ship.

A simple tune in ternary form, such as the famous Scottish air (with words by Robert Burns) "Ye Banks and Braes o' Bonnie Doon", repeats the "A" section.

A                              Ye banks and braes o' bonnie Doon,
                                 How can ye bloom sae fresh and fair?
                                 How can ye chaunt, ye little birds,
                                 And I'm sae weary fu' o' care?

B                              Ye'll break my heart, ye warbling bird
                               That warbles on the flow'ry thorn,

A                              Ye mind me o' departed joys,
                               Departed never to return.

From these simple structures emerges just about every musical form you can mention. Binary is a logical and satisfying structure, but it is less flexible, less expansive, less capable of development than ternary. In the history of music pieces of the binary type came before pieces of the ternary type. The history of western music is really about the developments possible for a composer who uses ternary form. But before the eighteenth and nineteenth centuries really showed us what could be done in three-part structures, masterpieces of many kinds were created in binary form.

The binary and ternary forms which so dominate musical thinking between 1600 and the present day, allow both sufficient exposure of the tune for the listener to be fully receptive, and also bring in that element of continuity and contrast previously mentioned. As we will see in later chapters, from the combination of main tune and subsidiary section come fruitful possibilities of development. It becomes possible for a composer to write a piece of music of satisfying substance which holds together as a unified work of art.

# 10

# Sacred Music

Music and words, as we have seen, go naturally together. The predominance of the human voice in music brings meaning and sound together. Words tend to shape and discipline music. In the realm of song (whether secular or religious), notes written by the composer must serve, support and enhance words. The sentiments of the text should be reinforced by music, making the words more immediately alive and vivid for the listener.

Singers must always be aware of the significance of words. This can only be achieved if the composer provides music entirely suitable for the chosen text. Fortunately composers through the ages have enjoyed the challenges posed by the setting of words to music. They have taken the task very seriously and never more so than when the text in question serves a religious purpose.

From the fusion of sacred words (whether Scripture, Missal or hymn) with the composer's art have come some of the great masterpieces of music. In particular the setting of the **Mass** has provided an extremely demanding musical form for composers to tackle. The five essential sections of the Mass commonly set by composers to music are the following:

(1)    *Kyrie, eleison* (Lord, have mercy)
(2)    *Gloria in excelsis Deo* (Glory be to God on high)
(3)    *Credo* (I believe)
(4)    *Sanctus* (Holy) with *Benedictus* (Blessing)
(5)    *Agnus Dei* (Lamb of God)

Palestrina's Mass for Pope Marcellus (Missa Papae Marcelli), J.S. Bach's Mass in B minor, Haydn's Theresa Mass, Mozart's Mass in C minor (K427), and Beethoven's Mass in D (Missa Solemnis) are some of the greatest achievements of European music.

Many composers have written a Mass for the Dead or Requiem. This is similar to the ordinary Mass but misses out the rejoicing of the *Gloria* and the *Credo*. It begins with the consoling words: *Requiem aeternam donna eis, Domine,* (Eternal rest grant unto them, O Lord), but includes the terrifying words of the *Dies Irae*: "That day, a day of wrath, of wasting, and of misery, a great day, and exceeding bitter." Palestrina, Mozart (on his deathbed), Berlioz, Verdi, Fauré and Dvořák were all inspired to write in this form.

An **oratorio**, written for performance in church, cathedral or (more recently) concert hall, is a large-scale work of devotion, putting a religious or exalted text to music. Handel's Messiah, one of the most popular of these, appears each Christmas as a regular part of the festivities. Haydn's Creation, Mendelssohn's Elijah, and Elgar's Dream of Gerontius (a setting of a religious poem by Cardinal Newman) are frequently performed oratorios.

The Easter season presents music of the Passion of Christ. A **Passion** is a setting of texts from the relevant passages in the Gospels or contemplative poems telling the story of Easter week. J.S. Bach's St Matthew Passion, written for an unprecedented array of soloists, double chorus, double orchestra, and organ, is the most colossal of these. Though first heard in 1729, it disappeared into silence for a century until brought back into performance by none other than Mendelssohn in 1829. Nowadays it is performed all over the world at Easter time.

Such mighty works must be considered as the equivalent of cathedrals in sound. The effect of attending a great performance of a sung Mass or oratorio is overwhelming. The purpose of sacred music, like that of a cathedral, is to express the highest religious aspirations of humanity. Though it is not necessary to share a religious faith to be able to appreciate these immense devotional works, the person of religious disposition must feel more at home with sacred music and its purpose. If we can admire both the architecture *and* the purpose of a cathedral, the significance of the place becomes two-fold. The intention of a religious work is primarily to elevate both a sacred text and a central belief. Yet even without belief, the works mentioned above offer a Niagaran torrent of magnificent sound. The melodious tumult of a choir and orchestra at the height of their powers in the resonant splendour of a great church cannot fail to move us.

Hymns and carols, the Gospel songs of the deep South of the USA (from which jazz partly originates), the intoning and chanting of prayer, and the communal music of worship, inspire in the listener feelings not evoked by any other kind of music. Religious music, whether it is Gregorian chant sung by a small choir or the mastery of Bach's St Matthew Passion, unleashes for composer and congregation a dimension of life which is still necessary. It is not so much for *listening to* as for *sharing in*. The function of sacred music is to create in us a mood quite different from everyday experience. For this reason it continues to exert considerable power over the imagination of composers. In the twentieth century great religious works, such as Stravinsky's Symphony of Psalms or Britten's War Requiem, continue the tradition of previous ages.

## Suggested listening

| | |
|---|---|
| 1525-94 | Palestrina, Giovanni Pierluigi da<br>Missa Papae Marcelli |
| 1567-1643 | Monteverdi, Claudio<br>Vespers of 1610 |
| 1685-1750 | Bach, Johann Sebastian<br>Mass in B minor St Matthew Passion |
| 1685-1759 | Handel, George Frideric<br>Messiah |
| 1732-1809 | Haydn, Joseph<br>The Creation |
| 1756-91 | Mozart, Wolfgang Amadeus<br>Requiem (K626) |
| 1770-1827 | Beethoven, Ludwig van<br>Mass in D Op.123 (Missa Solemnis) |
| 1803-69 | Berlioz, Hector<br>Grande Messe des Morts (Requiem Mass) |
| 1809-47 | Mendelssohn, Felix<br>Elijah |
| 1813-1901 | Verdi, Giuseppe<br>Requiem |
| 1857-1934 | Elgar, Edward<br>The Dream of Gerontius |
| 1882-1971 | Stravinsky, Igor<br>Symphony of Psalms |
| 1913-77 | Britten, Benjamin<br>A Ceremony of Carols<br>War Requiem |

# Music and Movement

Words, as we have seen, possess the ability to shape and define the forms of music. Folksong, sacred music, opera, blues and most kinds of popular entertainment would be unthinkable without the subtle intertwinings of sense and sound which occur when words and music meet.

Music without words is more abstract and sometimes more difficult to understand. It may make us feel happy, sad, joyous, funereal or stimulated. But music stripped of the spoken word has no necessity to limit itself to a precise statement of meaning. Music takes over where words leave off and can express those deep areas of feeling that are beyond words.

But music, as well as expressing different emotions, can also make us get up and dance. The graceful movements of the human body, the rhythms of the dancer, and the stylized routines of the ballroom have always been considered a worthy inspiration of music.

The power of the dance was enough for Herod to grant Salome whatever she should ask (her wish being the head of John the Baptist). Literature and legend abound in tales of heroines whose seductive dancing ensnares the vulnerable male, ranging from Morgiana in "Ali Baba and the Forty Thieves" to Carmen in Bizet's opera. When the dancer dances all eyes are riveted, and music becomes secondary to the dazzling display.

Dance music, therefore, must be simpler than pure instrumental music meant only for listening, and should not distract from the spectacle. The rhythmic movements of dancing feet and body impose restraint on the musician's imagination.

Historically, dance music is often divided between the vigorous energies of the countryside and the more refined temperament of the court. The essence of a country dance could pass quite naturally into the usage of courtly circles. As it did so, it became more formal and polite. The court musicians tended to polish the rough edges of a dance, making crude gusto elegant and transforming one style into another.

Then, following the whirligig of fashion, dances invariably drop out of popularity. At this point a peculiar thing may happen. Instrumental composers (of whom J.S. Bach is the supreme example) delighted in taking over a dance form where the dancers left off. When a dance is no longer as popular as it once was, it can then be exploited with great success as an instrumental form. Dance styles may endure for a short time only in the ballroom but they remain in people's memories long after their steps have been forgotten.

Modes of dress, etiquette, national temperament and prevailing influences are unpredictable weathercocks of contemporary taste. The rich and famous, especially those favoured at court, may influence the way the wind of fashion blows next, but try as they might, they cannot make fashion stand still. It is instrumental music, recreating the spirit of a dance form, which can preserve certain of its qualities for posterity, captured forever like a fly in amber.

# 12

# The Suite

Out of the traditions of dance emerged that most useful musical form the **Suite** (sometimes called **Partita**). As far as structure is concerned the suite is extremely uncomplicated. Out of assorted dances, each with a style, rhythm and mood of its own, a larger unity can be achieved. Put a few of these dances one after the other in a sequence, and they hang together like a necklace of precious stones; each item contributes to the overall effect yet each has its individual identity.

The suite reached its zenith in the works of J.S. Bach, who wrote them for solo instruments — violin, 'cello, keyboard and lute. He also composed suites for orchestra though these followed patterns and structures somewhat different from the instrumental suites with which we are concerned here.

Enjoyable listening to the suite depends once again on expectations. Knowledge of each movement improves understanding. Without some idea of what a dance sets out to do, the effect can be blurred and even tedious.

The origins of the suite are believed to be in the habit of pairing a slow dance (with four or two beats to the bar) such as the Pavane, with a quicker dance (with three beats to the bar) such as a Galliard. This is a logical progression from a stately, elegant pace to a more exciting climax.

Throughout the seventeenth century composers experimented with notions of the suite. The perfection of the form that we associate with J.S. Bach was not reached easily. Like cards in a pack, the available dances were constantly shuffled. The possible permutations of dances fascinated composers, who took their time to evolve a suitable climactic and expressive sequence.

Johann Jacob Froberger (1616-67) is often acknowledged as the "father of the suite". He wrote several suites consisting of allemande-courante-sarabande, and others that placed a gigue between allemande and courante. J.S. Bach's instrumental suites, though they vary in actual choice of dances, settled basically around the following pattern:

allemande — courante — sarabande — minuet — gigue
(slow)        (quick)        (slow)        (quick)    (very quick)

To this outline can be added prelude, bourrée, gavotte, passepied, loure, variations (known as doubles), and other items such as scherzo, burlesca, caprice, rondeau, etc. To the uninitiated listener the suite could become a labyrinth of dance types, each as archaic as all the others. But information about the parts of the structure reveals that the suite is actually a miniature drama containing its own logic.

The opening of the suite is always important. Like the beginning of a novel or film the first moments suggest the mood of the entire work. Whether Bach begins with a prelude or allemande, or an ouverture or fantasie, the effect is to draw the attention of player and listener. Most of the suite will stay in one key. A suite is often referred to in terms of its tonality. A "Suite in E minor" will have a very distinct mood compared with a "Suite in A major", and the function of the first few bars will be to establish something of the musical atmosphere to be expected.

A **prelude** is an introduction to the suite in a free style of writing with no fixed rules. It is in this way unlike most of the movements of the suite which have two distinct sections in true binary shape. The composer's imagination can be let loose in the prelude, exploring avenues not possible in the dance forms to follow.

An **allemande**, a dance of German origin as its name implies, suggests the fluid smoothness of untroubled waters. Its four beats in a bar give it stability and the number of notes indicate ease and fluency. The pace of this dance is quiet and steady, not brilliant. For this reason Bach often starts his suite with an allemande. In a suite opening with a prelude, the allemande provides a useful second movement. The initial qualities suggested by the prelude can be extended by the allemande without giving away too much of the drama to follow.

The **courante**, however, is vigorous and rapid, providing a contrast to the allemande. From the French verb "to run", the courante is a bubbling, effervescent stream, hurtling downhill. It may not always be profound but it is usually brilliant.

The slow **sarabande**, which probably originated in Spain, is the deep lake into which the running courante tumbles! It contains enormous depths of stillness, sadness and expressiveness. Its three beats to the bar are unusual since (like the Polish mazurka) the middle beat of the three is often the accented one:

$$1 \quad \overset{>}{2} \quad 3 \quad / \quad 1 \quad \overset{>}{2} \quad 3$$

The sarabande is the centrifugal point of the suite. To this, all dances move, and from this all subsequent movements retreat.

**Minuets, gavottes**, and **bourrées** remind us, in their rhythmic simplicity, of the true dance. Their life is very physical and springy, quite removed from the soulful anguish of the sarabande. After the beauty of reflection, they bring us back to reality and simple pleasures. They lack the sophistication of allemandes and courantes, and release us from the introspective gravity of the sarabande. The minuet is a graceful movement with three beats to a bar, sometimes followed by a second minuet. The gavotte is bright in mood and starts halfway through the first bar providing a catchy rhythm and is also sometimes followed by a second gavotte. Occasionally this second gavotte is in the form of a **musette**, a dance with a drone bass that imitates the sound of the bagpipe, an instrument popular in France and after which the movement is named. The bourrée is another French dance, similar to the gavotte but quicker. It can be followed by a second bourrée and in some instances the first bourrée is then repeated.

The **gigue** has many virtues. It generates excitement, vigour and zest with a foot-tapping rhythm. Yet its textures are often complex, with interwoven voices, making considerable demands on the player's dexterity. This is where the suite comes to a dramatic culmination. The gigue is probably descended from the English jig, the characteristic rhythm of which still persists.

In J.S. Bach's suites these contrasts of excitement and serenity, joy and sadness, intensity and relaxation are fully exploited. The massive "architecture" of his suites and the great emotional sweep of the overall design have never been equalled. Bach, above all other composers, showed us what the suite could achieve.

#### Suggested listening

| | |
|---|---|
| 1659-95 | Purcell, Henry<br>Suites for Harpsichord |
| 1685-1750 | Bach, Johann Sebastian<br>French Suites for keyboard<br>6 Suites for Solo 'Cello |
| 1685-1759 | Handel, George Frideric<br>Suites for keyboard |

# Rondeau, Rondo

One of the earliest dance forms which demonstrates the meta-morphosis of musical shape and function is the group round dance. For men and women to join hands and dance in a closed circle is an ancient form of dance. The accompaniment was provided by the voice singing a chorus or refrain which returned after each verse.

This round dance became a popular medieval form, the **rondeau**, beloved by troubadours, jongleurs and minstrels. Instruments were added to fill out the vocal line and the rondeau ultimately passed from the lips of poets and singers to the fingers of instrumentalists. It became an invaluable musical structure for later composers, infusing the qualities of repetition with new con-trasting material.

By the time of Haydn, Mozart and Beethoven, **rondo** (now called by its Italian name) was both a solo instrumental form and had also developed into a useful movement of the sonata. The latter is often referred to as being in **sonata rondo** form. The pattern of rondo thus became either:

A    B    A    C    A

or:

A    B    A    C    A    B    A

Here, A represents the principal melody, B and C represent the intermediate sections often referred to as **episodes**. It will be observed that the second example in particular has a definite ternary shape. This fact was especially attractive to composers of the eighteenth and nineteenth centuries.

Thus the history of the rondeau endures from ancient times right up to the present day for twentieth century composers still use rondo form. For the most part, rondos retain a mood of vigour which suggests a legacy from the early dance.

Even though the rondo has become primarily an instrumental work, the dance itself survives, often with sung chorus and verses, in children's games, folk gatherings and party activities such as the boisterous "hokey-cokey". The magic circle of joined hands continues to fascinate.


## Suggested listening

| 1668-1733 | Couperin, François |
| | Rondeau from 8th Ordre in B minor |

1756-91      Mozart, Wolfgang Amadeus
Rondo in A minor (K511)
Sonata in C(K545), last movement

1770-1827      Beethoven, Ludwig van
Sonata in C Op. 53 ("Waldstein") last movement
Sonata in G Op. 79 (Alla tedesca), last movement

1810-56      Schumann, Robert
Arabeske Op. 18

# 14

# Theme and Variations

Words and dance, as we have seen, impart to music their own structure. They support patterns of music like pillars in a temple, making the form logical, coherent and strong. But what happens when music relies neither on text nor dance rhythms but goes instead towards the realm of "pure music"?

One of the composer's solutions to the difficulties of shaping music in the abstract, or **absolute music** as it is called (i.e. consisting only of music with no reference to anything outside itself) is to write **variations on a theme**. The idea is simplicity itself. To carry out the intention is not so straightforward.

For a start a composer should be passionately fond of the melody, whether original or borrowed, and be committed to the theme with a firm belief in its musical possibilities. In the sixteenth and seventeenth centuries it was usual to select a stock theme from the popular melodies of the day. In more recent times composers have been expected to create their own basis for variations by writing a really inspired, memorable and catchy opening. The melody selected should be concise and immediately attractive. If the listener has not grasped the theme by the time it has been played, the variations that follow will be meaningless. This important principle of all musical shape — that what comes first must be absorbed thoroughly to make sense of what follows — is particularly vital in variation form.

The melody at the heart of the variations, though attractive, is evidently not self-sufficient. It is the starting point of a longer work. The mood is set by it, and this gives rise to a sequence of other moods. Yet, at every point during the subsequent variations, the listener, consciously or subconsciously, possesses in imagination the substance of the original tune.

A framework for a set of "free" variations (where no constraints are imposed on the composer's imagination) could be built up in many ways. But in a typical set of variations a musical form is set in motion along the following lines.

After the statement of the theme the first variation, though harking back to the tune, brings us in direct contact with the composer's inventive ability. Therefore it is frequently assertive and striking. The composer does not need to get too near the theme as we have only just heard it played.

What follows rings the changes. Variations can come faster or slower, softer or louder, more dissonant or more consonant, near or far from the melody, in major or minor keys. Faster variations may well be placed strategically next to slower ones (as we have already seen with the suite). But each moment takes us further from the original melody in time and distance, and deeper into an experience the composer has created. The theme gives the initial impetus — the variations provide depth and intensity.

Within the theme and variations must be a definite sense of progress. The last variation is usually an impressive finale. On occasion it could even be a repeat of the tune itself, the journey then being a round trip, from the home ground and back again via fascinating scenery. But whatever happens we pass through a sequence of musical events, ranging from the first simple statement of the theme to a deeper process of exploration.

So far the theme and variations form has been considered as it mainly appeared later on in musical history — as a free form giving the composer ample scope to exercise full choice in the matter. Composers have certainly taken advantage of the indulgence afforded by the variation form. Elgar, in his "Enigma" Variations, after a superb and original opening melody presents character sketches in music of fourteen people (including a self portrait in the Finale).

Benjamin Britten's Nocturnal, written for the guitar, surprises us by leaving the actual theme, "Come Heavy Sleep" by John Dowland, to the end of the composition. The many moods of sleep are evoked throughout the variations, indicated by the composer's instructions to the player — "musingly", "agitated", "restless", "uneasy" and "dreaming".

In earlier sets of variations composers inflicted a more severe discipline on themselves, amounting almost to a musical straitjacket. Freedom of the kind espoused by later musicians was less in favour. The pattern was established in such works by a scrupulous observation, not of the tune, but of its harmonies, and in particular the bottom line of the harmony.

Taking the bass, or **ground**, of a tune, the composer constructed on the actual foundations of the piece a new superstructure. The ground was repeated time after time, and against this unwavering repetition, the composer was invited to pit his wits. The results were often amazingly refreshing and inventive. From the variations on a ground, spring those remarkable species of musical shape, the **passacaglia** and the **chaconne**. (J.S. Bach's Chaconne in D minor for solo violin remains the zenith of this form; and a splendid example of the Passacaglia is the last movement of Brahms's Fourth Symphony where he weaves thirty different variations on a theme taken from a Bach Cantata.)

The fascination of these more rigid variation forms lies in watching the composer evade the obvious limitations. In using this particular structure, the composer becomes an artistic Houdini, constantly escaping from the tediousness which threatens a musician who dares to repeat himself too often.

Traditional jazz, with its improvised choruses over an established sequence of chords (musicians improvising on the harmonies, not the tune), contains many of the elements of the chaconne and passacaglia idea. Composers and improvisers have discovered many times how imagination flourishes when it is subject to a carefully created structure. Musical anarchy is seldom satisfying to performer or listener. For this reason the variation form, whether free or in the passacaglia mould, will continue to challenge composers.

## Suggested listening

1583-1643 Frescobaldi, Girolamo
Air with Variations on "La Frescobalda"

1685-1750 Bach, Johann Sebastian
Chaconne from Partita No. 2 in D minor
for Solo Violin
Goldberg Variations for harpsichord

1685-1759 Handel, George Frideric
"The Harmonious Blacksmith" (Air and Variations
from Suite No. 5 for harpsichord)

1732-1809 Haydn, Joseph
Variations in F minor (Hob.XVII/6) for piano

| 1756-91 | Mozart, Wolfgang Amadeus |
|---|---|
| | (1st movement of Piano Sonata in A (K331) |
| | 12 Variations on "Ah, vous dirai-je maman" |
| | (K265) for piano |

| 1770-1827 | Beethoven, Ludwig van |
|---|---|
| | Diabelli Variations Op. 120 for piano |
| | 32 Variations in C minor for piano |

| 1797-1828 | Schubert, Franz |
|---|---|
| | 4th movement of Piano Quintet in A — |
| | "The Trout" (D667) |
| | Piano Impromptu No. 3 Op.142 (D935) |

| 1822-90 | Franck, César |
|---|---|
| | Symphonic Variations for Piano and Orchestra |

| 1833-97 | Brahms, Johannes |
|---|---|
| | Variations and Fugue on a Theme by Handel Op.24 |
| | Variations on a Theme by Paganini Op.35 |
| | Last movement of Symphony No.4 in E minor Op.98 |
| | St Anthony Variations Op.56a |

| 1857-1934 | Elgar, Edward |
|---|---|
| | Variations on an Original Theme ("Enigma") Op.36 |

| 1873-1943 | Rachmaninov, Sergei |
|---|---|
| | Rhapsody on a Theme of Paganini |

| 1877-1960 | Dohnányi, Ernst von |
|---|---|
| | Variations on a Nursery Song Op.25 |

| 1913-77 | Britten, Benjamin |
|---|---|
| | Nocturnal after John Dowland for guitar Op.70 |
| | Variations on a Theme of Frank Bridge Op.10 |
| | Young Person's Guide to the Orchestra Op.34 |

# 15

# Fugue

Certain types of structure in music fascinate composers of widely differing historical periods. The challenge in such instances is taken up again and again by musicians eager to confront the severest tests of their vocation.

Thus the attraction of **fugue** spans several centuries. It is a medium which never seems to become obsolete. Certainly the glorious years of the polyphonic tradition culminated in J.S. Bach, the Grand Master of all fugue; his organ fugues, the Forty-eight Preludes and Fugues for the Well-tempered Klavier (written to demonstrate the effectiveness of a new type of tuning known as equal temperament which has been in use ever since), and the *Art of Fugue* are some of his greatest masterpieces. Yet fortunately Bach's genius in this field did not inhibit later composers from attempting to write fugues.

The fugal choruses in Handel's Messiah, Mozart's double fugue in his Requiem, Beethoven's *Grosse Fuge* Op. 133 for String Quartet, the fugue at the end of his Hammerklavier Sonata, and the double fugue in the Ninth Symphony are some of the finest manifestations of the form. Others include Mendelssohn's Six Preludes and Fugues (1837), Liszt's Piano Sonata in B minor (1854) which includes elements of fugue, Brahms's Variations and Fugue on a Theme by Handel Op. 24 (1861), and César Franck's Prelude, Choral and Fugue for piano. In the twentieth century Paul Hindemith's Ludus Tonalis (1943) brings to mind Bach's "Forty-eight" in a work consisting of twelve fugues in twelve keys, linked by interludes, plus prelude and postlude; Dmitri Shostakovich's Twenty-four Preludes and Fugues Op. 87 for keyboard (finished in 1951) also provide a significant modern contribution to fugal tradition.

To write a successful fugue the composer must become a kind of musical juggler. A number of melodic fragments are flung up in the air and must be kept in harmonious balance simultaneously. If one tune drops limply to the ground whilst others remain aloft, the result is artistic failure.

The composer begins the fugue by throwing one small melody into action. This keeps going whilst another voice joins in. A third part enters the fray as existing parts continue to wing along. The composer can keep on adding ingredients to the mixture, but like the juggler, the more flaming torches that are tossed up, the greater the risk of disaster.

Fugue is quite straightforward when each part is distributed among individual singers or sections of a choir. Trebles, altos, tenors and basses, interweaving lines of melody enable the listener to hear each voice easily. If the fugue is spread between various orchestral instruments the same applies.

But composers were eager to demonstrate fugal skills in other ways. They applied fugue to solo music, writing not only for organ (which was ideal, having more than one keyboard, pedal basses, and an ability to imitate differing instrumental sounds) but also to harpsichord, violin and lute, with magnificent results.

The inherent problems of fugue composition take us into the realm of pure mathematics. Lines of moving melody can easily collide with catastrophic results. The art of fugue is to write music so expertly that not a blemish occurs. Adjacent melodies must cohere and agree like a happy family, and any sudden quarrel should be speedily resolved.

As a species, the fugue is elusive and independent, but if a hundred fugues by various composers (and especially the Forty-eight Preludes and Fugues of Bach) were to be pinned down on a board like butterflies and dissected, certain principles would emerge. Over the years an extensive vocabulary of terms has been developed to describe and analyse the fugue.

Fugues have recognizable beginnings, middles and endings, which could be set out in the following way:

1) **The Opening** (known as **The Exposition**)

(a) The first voice brings in the theme, known as the **Subject**. This is in the tonic or home key.

(b) The second voice answers the Subject, pitched a fifth higher or a fourth lower than the first voice. While the **Answer** is sounding, the first voice sings a **Countersubject**, a melody which blends appropriately with the Answer.

(c) The third voice enters with the Subject in the original key. First and second voices provide suitable Countersubjects.

(d) A fourth voice (if there is one) comes in with the

Answer, once more in the dominant. The Countersubjects sing on in the other voices meanwhile.

One by one, voices have joined the game of fugue. Each entry momentarily hogs the limelight and its individual contribution is firmly established. Once each part has been adequately introduced the fugue can move to the next stage of development.

## 2)  The Middle

The fugue now leaves the tonic key laid down at the opening, and modulates to new tonalities. Subject and Answer can sing their original parts in a fresh key, or little sections of music, called **Episodes**, can divert momentarily from the repetition of Subject and Answer. Once the delights of novel material and contrasting episodic interludes are exhausted, the composer can turn towards home and a triumphant finale.

## 3)  The Ending

When the Middle stops and the Ending begins is not always clear. One sign of an impending climax might be the return of Subject and Answer in the tonic key. In the Exposition, Subject and Answer were separated to allow each part to establish its own presence. The composer now brings Subject and Answer closer together, a device known as **Stretto** (from the Italian — drawing together). At this point the fugal texture may be densely populated. The voices crowd in like an excitable conversation where everyone speaks at the same time without waiting for others to finish what they have to say.

A **Coda** or tail is often added after these final statements to round off the fugue with a craftsmanlike flourish.

These are the guidelines of fugue, though they cannot encompass the mass of detail which such a composition contains. It has often been acknowledged that fugue is not so much a form as a texture, the intermingling of polyphonic lines of sound. Yet out of this mathematical conundrum of voice pitted against voice against voice (etc.), truly remarkable fabrics of sound emerge.

A fugue compels the listener to concentrate. Real participation is needed as the ear switches its focus from one voice to another. In fugue the composer is not only a brilliant juggler of melodies but becomes a wizard weaving spells, a mathematician solving problems and a conjurer revealing amazing musical tricks. Few other types of form make such a total demand on the listener's attention. Not only is there a great art in the composition and performance of fugues — but also in listening to them.

## Suggested listening

| | |
|---|---|
| 1685-1750 | Bach, Johann Sebastian<br>*The Art of Fugue*<br>Toccata and Fugue in D minor<br>(BWV565) for organ<br>The Well-Tempered Klavier<br>(48 Preludes and Fugues) |
| 1685-1759 | Handel, George Frideric<br>Amen Chorus from the "Messiah" |
| 1770-1827 | Beethoven, Ludwig van<br>Grosse Fuge Op.133 |
| 1895-1963 | Hindemith, Paul<br>Ludus Tonalis |
| 1906-75 | Shostakovich, Dmitri<br>24 Preludes and Fugues for piano Op.87 |

# 16

# Sonata

The **sonata** is one of music's most ingenious discoveries. Like the development of the novel or the camera, it opened up new worlds of artistic exploration. Moreover the sonata was uniquely flexible above all other musical forms in the sense that it could include movements such as variations, minuets, fugues and rondos. Sonata became a recognizable structure with its own special identity; composers could adapt that structure for their own purposes without destroying its essential spirit.

Originally the word "sonata" meant little more than "sounded" (from the Italian) as opposed to "cantata" meaning "sung". From the sixteenth century composers applied the term freely to many kinds of music written for instruments. Eventually however, a sonata began to mean a particular species of instrumental work in three or four movements. This process began to establish itself around 1742 when Carl Philipp Emanuel Bach, the second surviving son of J.S. Bach, published his first book of (for the most part) three movement sonatas.

Before C.P.E. Bach the most renowned composer of keyboard sonatas was Domenico Scarlatti (1685-1757). He wrote over five hundred one-movement sonatas, set out in two balanced halves, similar to the double sections of a dance movement in a suite. This straightforward structure follows a pattern which served Scarlatti very well:

First half     A     A strong melody in the tonic key advances to the dominant key by the end of the section. This half is then repeated to give the listener a second chance to absorb and enjoy it.

Second half   B     The music begins in the dominant key, and moves back to the tonic key at the end of the section. This second half is also repeated providing a structure of symmetry, balance and order.

While Scarlatti's sonatas are still popular, the works of C.P.E. Bach tend to be neglected by the recitalists of today. Yet the concepts of musical structure they reveal proved to be extremely influential.

The pattern of these prototype sonatas set a precedent. The three movements followed a routine of contrasting moods and speeds:

| | |
|---|---|
| First movement: | Quick |
| Second movement: | Slow or very slow |
| Third movement: | Very quick |

The second movement was usually set in a contrasting key (such as the relative minor) and it consisted of just one section, reminiscent of the freedom of the prelude in a suite. This slow movement explored a serious and sensitive mood that did not have to follow any preordained rules. (It is similar to the fantasia, a free form also much liked by C.P.E. Bach as an expressive style.) This element of freedom in the slow movement became a characteristic aspect of sonatas.

On either side of the slow movement, the quicker movements stood sentinel. They were often in binary form with each half repeated. Here, C.P.E. Bach sometimes introduced not just one theme in the typical Scarlatti or suite convention, but allowed a suggestion of a second theme to enter. This deployment of two melodies was to set the seal on sonata. Between two themes in one movement, a spark could leap, generating energy and development, fusion and diversity.

C.P.E. Bach's sonatas developed throughout his lifetime in length, variety and sensitivity. As well as the form of his works composers admired his music's emotional content. C.P.E. Bach as possible. . . . As I see it, music should move the heart emotionally. . . .

> My chief study, particularly in later years, has been directed towards playing *clavier* . . . so that playing should be as much like singing as possible. . . . As I see it, music should move the heart emotionally. . . .

The sonata became indeed one of the most deeply emotional of all musical forms. It was the structure which shaped string quartets, symphonies, and concertos, as well as pieces written for soloists and for instruments playing in partnership, from the eighteenth century to the present day. The tributary of C.P.E.

Bach's music thus flowed directly towards the great river of compositions by Haydn, Mozart, Beethoven and Schubert.

The eighteenth century is the great watershed of music. At that time new textures, new forms and new instruments were developed and the world of music was never the same again. After 1750, the year of J.S. Bach's death, the period known to musical history as the Baroque gently gives way to the era which we call Classical.

In 1749, Joseph Haydn (1732-1809) rented a garret and playing on "an old worm-eaten clavier" studied the six early sonatas of C.P.E. Bach. Continuity in music is thus maintained. Some quality in an older composer's music appeals to a young musician and teaches him lessons which may never be forgotten. Haydn in his turn was to be the highly esteemed older friend of Wolfgang Amadeus Mozart (1756-91) and even the teacher, for a short time, of Ludwig van Beethoven (1770-1827). These three composers between them transformed the structure and concept of European music.

In 1755 Haydn became music master to the family of Baron Joseph von Fürnberg, and soon after wrote his first attempts at the **string quartet** (which is like a sonata but played not by one instrument but by four — two violins, viola and 'cello). Haydn composed over eighty string quartets altogether, a musical medium which he initiated, and which Mozart and Beethoven continued. (It was through the string quartet that he developed many of the principles of **sonata form** which we will deal with in the next chapter.)

String quartets are a musical testing-ground where a composer can write intimate music and experiment with lines of sound. Such music can appeal to players even more than to listeners. If we attend a concert by a string quartet we overhear the music, whereas with a symphony the music speaks outwardly and directly to us. Compared with orchestral music, a string quartet is an economical form of composition, and performances can be arranged with little formality.

The texture of a string quartet is that of utmost clarity and unity. It is the closest thing in music to a conversation. The voices of a string quartet are like independent speakers, each contributing to the overall design.

After a certain amount of exploration in his early quartets, Haydn eventually settled on a four movement sequence. This organization became characteristic and convenient for subsequent composers right up to the present day. The sonata (as it had now developed), the string quartet, the symphony and the concerto all follow the contours of this pattern:

| | |
|---|---|
| First movement: (quick) | The most important movement in that it establishes themes, mood and content. |
| Second movement: (slow) | A lyrical movement, usually in a different key from the first movement. |
| Third movement: (fairly quick) | This consists of a relic of the dance suite; two Minuets are played, the second one being entitled the **Trio** (named after the early custom of using three instruments only in this section in order to obtain greater contrast with the first minuet.) After the Trio has been played the first Minuet comes again. (The Minuet eventually quickened its speed and turned into a **Scherzo** — the Italian for "joke", thus indicating its change of character to a lighter mood. Beethoven is considered the principal initiator of the scherzo.) |
| Fourth movement: (quick or very quick) | This is energetic, exuberant and full of strong rhythms making an exciting finish. |

Every string quartet, every sonata, every symphony, makes up its own rules to some extent. So if the first movement was not very quick or lively, Haydn could put the Minuet and Trio before the slow movement, thus subtly altering the dramatic shape of the piece. The outline is not a prison for the composer's imagination, but a dynamic framework which expands and lives in response to the life breathed into it. Such a structure offers a composer every advantage to shape a coherent musical pattern within which many moods can be created.

The advantage of the sonata pattern could be summed up as follows:

1) The composer can use contrasts in tonality throughout the four movements. The home key established strongly in the

first movement becomes the foil for tonal surprises, novelties, and even shocks. The listener is delighted by shifts in tonality, even if not quite sure in musical language what is happening.

2) The four movements between them give plenty of differentiation in rhythm and pace, as well as volume and intensity.

3) Each movement can be shaped individually yet the four movements still cohere through the binding force of tonality and the composer's imaginative moulding of melodic and harmonic elements.

4) The ebbing and flowing of the musical tide culminates in the excitement of the finale. The four movements progress in dramatic sequence towards a logical climax.

# 17

# Sonata Form

The first movement in our overall sonata pattern has a form of its own known as **sonata form** or **first-movement form**. Here is what happens in the first movement of a sonata, string quartet or symphony:

The first movement is divided into three parts, the opening, the middle, and the ending.

The opening, or **Exposition**

The composer thinks of a good melody to begin his sonata. The melody is firmly in the tonic key, and is immediately significant and memorable. This opening theme is called the **First Subject**.

Between the First Subject and what follows is a short linking section called the **Bridge Passage**; this gives us the clue to get ready for new events.

Following the successful statement of the First Subject, the composer thinks of another tune. This is in the dominant (or related) key; the effect of this melody is to give us a change of scenery and lead us a little way from home. The second melody is known as the **Second Subject**.

The whole of the Exposition is then repeated to make sure that the messages conveyed by the First and Second Subjects are fully grasped. Nowadays, when records and cassettes have the power to give us great familiarity with a work, a performer of a keyboard sonata sometimes omits this repeat. However, the architecture of this first movement form really demands the repeat to drive home the essential landmarks. Without these landmarks the sonata will be less meaningful.

The middle section or
**Development**

The composer selects various aspects from the Exposition and explores and elaborates their musical possibilities. The Development does not have to be long or complicated, though it could be. The imaginative use of modulation from one key to another is one of a multitude of possibilities.

The ending or **Recapitulation**

To bring us back home the First Subject is played again. We hear it with experienced ears, having passed through the rigours of the Development. Reaching home after an adventurous journey means that we are not the same as when we set out. The tonic key reassures us that the promised land could be near.

Another **Bridge Passage** eases us from the dominance of the First Subject towards the return of the Second Subject.

The Second Subject returns like an old acquaintance. But now it is more friendly, being in the tonic key (it was previously in the dominant). In the company of this welcome guide we arrive at the end of the first movement. To emphasize a sense of home-coming a final Coda is sometimes added.

When watching a play, audiences recognize individual characters, and know which act is in progress. The manoeuvres of the plot will be keenly observed, and the climax looked forward to with warm expectation. A musical structure in sonata form needs listeners who can participate similarly.

## Suggested listening

| | |
|---|---|
| 1685-1757 | Scarlatti, Domenico<br>Keyboard Sonatas |
| 1714-88 | Bach, Carl Philipp Emanuel<br>Keyboard Sonatas |
| 1732-1809 | Haydn, Joseph<br>Keyboard Sonatas<br>String Quartets |
| 1756-91 | Mozart, Wolfgang Amadeus<br>Piano Sonata in C (K545)<br>Piano Sonata in A minor (K310)<br>**String Quartet No. 17 in Bb (K458), "The Hunt"**<br>String Quartet No. 19 in C (K465), "The Dissonance" |
| 1770-1827 | Beethoven, Ludwig van<br>Piano Sonata in F minor Op.57, "Appassionata"<br>Piano Sonata in C minor Op. 13, "Pathétique"<br>Sonata for Violin and Piano in A Op.47, "Kreutzer"<br>Piano Trio in Bb Op.97, "Archduke"<br>String Quartets Op.59 "Rasumovsky" |
| 1797-1828 | Schubert, Franz<br>Piano Sonata in Bb (D960)<br>Octet in F (D803) for Wind and Strings<br>String Quintet in C (D956) |

# 18

# Symphony

The problems of listening to a **symphony** are not easy to solve. It requires the equivalent, in terms of mental energy, of watching a long play such as *Hamlet* or *King Lear*. Though smaller symphonies, lighter in texture, are available, larger blockbuster symphonies demand great attention from their audiences. Symphonies lasting over forty minutes are plentiful, and these require almost Herculean concentration from the listener.

In the concert hall the symphony is presented at its most exciting. The presence of the orchestra, the mighty wash of sound, the fascination of the occasion and the silence of the audience, enclose the listener in a cocoon ideal for paying attention to the music.

The sheer volume of a large orchestra, as well as the energy and variation of orchestral colours, has a profound effect on the nervous system. As the music proceeds through the various movements — quick, slow, minuet (or scherzo) and trio, and the finale — the audience is carried along on a vast sea of vibrating sound. Even a complete lack of interest in the form of a symphony cannot destroy the sense of excitement and pulsating energy as a full orchestra plays for all its worth.

The symphony concert represents a truly dramatic event. The characters in the drama consist of conductor, musicians and audience, all interacting with each other to provide atmosphere and tension. The dress suits of the players, the movements of the conductor, and the disciplined unity of the orchestra give a striking visual dimension which is very important.

A great symphony is meant to stimulate involvement throughout its entirety. It presents many moods, including fantasy, verve, silence, joy, sadness, wildness and sometimes just good solid themes. The moments of intensity come intermittently; at other times a gentle languor can settle for a short while over audience and orchestra alike, the lull before the storm, or the postlude to passion.

In the concert hall the music hits the audience in the face. Facing the source of the sound, unable to move about, the listener takes in the full experience. Stimulation towards listening closely is at its highest in this context.

At home, through radio or record player, the symphony speaks in another way. This is the ideal way to become acquainted with the details of individual movements, to listen to certain passages over and over again. Though the rewards of intimate knowledge of a work are immense, it does take considerable self-discipline to sit down in the privacy of one's home to attend closely and without distraction to a long symphony all the way through.

How the symphony originally came into being is a topic much discussed by musicologists. G.B. Sammartini (1698-75), C.P.E. Bach (1714-88), G.C. Wagenseil (1715-77), Johann Stamitz (1717-57), F.J. Gossec (1734-1829), J.C. Bach (1735-82), etc. all took part in the early development of what we now think of as the symphony. Taking their cue from the form of the Italian overture with three contrasting movements, they began to evolve a quite distinctive and indeed revolutionary type of orchestral work.

**Overtures** to operas are works which create an appropriate atmosphere for the drama to follow. Yet, overtures are often substantial enough in their own right to merit performances in the concert hall quite removed from the opera they were intended to preface. Popular overtures of the late seventeenth century were of two types — French or Italian. Each possessed three movements, the French preferring a slow-quick-slow pattern, whilst the Italian overture with quick-slow-quick was clearly related to sonata shape. It was the latter which attracted the attention of the early symphonists

Many composers and many shifts of fashion contributed to the gradual development of symphonic sound. The work, for example, of superb violinists such as Lully (1632-87) and Corelli (1653-1713) completed the process of displacing the viols as the favourite bowed instrument. Viols, bowed instruments with frets used in small chamber groups, had been popular for centuries. The predominance of the violin family ensured not only the ultimate departure of the viols but established up to the present day the primary textures of orchestral sound. For the characteristic sound of symphony is essentially the sound of violins and their relatives, the viola, 'cello and double bass; these dominate in no uncertain terms the structure of the orchestra, and without their rise to this central position the symphony might never have existed.

Symphony developed as a sonata in orchestral clothing. The typical symphony follows the patterns of sonata outlined in Chapters 16 and 17. But as well as its form, we must always think of its characteristic sound, a quality which pervades symphonies from the early eighteenth century to the modern age. Musical structure in terms of movement and theme is at one here with the composer's delight in mixing the tone colours of various families of instruments against the relatively constant flow of bowed sound. In their symphonies composers were able to pursue endlessly the complexities of musical chemistry — the combining of bowed string elements with woodwind, brass and percussion. This process eventually involved a steady expansion of the size, range and capabilities of the orchestra.

The first great composer to write powerfully in symphonic form was Joseph Haydn, often called the "father of the symphony". His advocacy of the newly fledged symphony helped the form find its musical feet. He wrote no less than 104 symphonies, thereby setting an influential precedent for other composers.

These symphonies established for all time the basic ground rules for the structure. His masterpieces in this genre are four movement works of great variety and vivacity. Apart from a slow introduction which precedes the quick first movement, a device which successfully captures the audience's attention, Haydn's symphonies follow the patterns of the sonata and string quartet as described in the previous chapter.

His symphonies have often been given picturesque titles: Symphony No. 94 in G, "The Surprise" — a sudden very loud chord surprises the gentle flow of the slow movement; Symphony No. 100 in G, "The Military" — one of the Salomon symphonies which contains a military sounding trumpet, bass drum etc. (Salomon was a concert promoter who lived in London and organized Haydn's visits to England. The twelve symphonies he wrote for these occasions are known as the Salomon symphonies.); Symphony No. 101 in D, "The Clock" — the ticking of a clock is suggested in the slow movement; Symphony No. 103 in E flat, "The Drum-Roll" — opens with a roll on the kettledrum; Symphony No. 45 in F sharp minor, "The Farewell", in the last movement of which each musician in turn stops playing. These are some of the symphonies of Haydn with names which make them easily identifiable. (The addition of a colourful name to a symphony has helped to popularize many compositions in this form: Beethoven's "Eroica" — heroic — intended for

Napoleon, although Beethoven later changed his mind on hearing that the great man had declared himself emperor; Schubert's "Unfinished" — it contains only two movements; Mendelssohn's "Italian" — inspired by a visit there; Tchaikovsky's "Pathétique" — indicating its mood; Dvořák's "New World" — written in and inspired by America; and Shostakovich's "Leningrad" — depicting that city under siege during the Second World War; all are well-known examples.)

Haydn's symphonies are energetic and witty, as well as beauti-ful and serene. They are more compact and succinct than some of the longer symphonies of later composers and as superbly enjoyable music they will always hold their place in the repertoire of works frequently performed.

Mozart's symphonies (over forty in number) create a somewhat different frame of mind from those of Haydn. The profound expressiveness of the symphony is fully exploited by Mozart with more disturbing undercurrents than we normally associate with Haydn. On the surface Mozart's music may seem as smooth and perfect as a sparkling sea but beneath that elegant exterior there is an underlying seriousness and sometimes a sense of tragedy. Haydn blueprinted and established the great musical machine known as "symphony", but Mozart fine-tuned it and made it capable of a greater emotional charge. Mozart poured light and shade, tension and vigour, anguish and brilliance, into the symphonic mould. His symphonies opened up new dimensions and expanded musical horizons.

For the public at large Ludwig van Beethoven (1770-1827) remains the supreme symphonist. His symphonies are bigger, louder and longer than those of either Haydn or Mozart, and they are also fewer in number, being restricted to the magical figure of nine. After the first two symphonies, the Third, the "Eroica" as its name implies, is on a truly heroic scale. It contains a sombre Funeral March, and an impulsive Scherzo, while the Finale combines variation and fugue forms. Beethoven's Fifth remains the most universally popular of all symphonies. The arresting opening four notes constitute probably the most famous of all symphonic phrases. His Ninth, as well as being the first symphony to introduce the human voice, is also the most epic. It became known as the "Choral" Symphony as in the last movement Beethoven sets a part of Schiller's "Ode to Joy" for solo singers and chorus. With Beethoven the entire concept of the symphony involves mountainous peaks of human and artistic endeavour. By the time of his Ninth the orchestra had expanded into a mighty phalanx of sound with a rich array of resources.

Just as J.S. Bach set the highest criterion among composers in his writing of fugue, so Beethoven's symphonies have come to be regarded as the touchstone for all symphonies. Later composers, such as Schubert and Brahms, contemplated Beethoven's achievements with awe and regarded him as the supreme master of symphony.

Symphony is such a remarkably satisfying musical structure that composers have continued to write in this form up to the present day. Since Beethoven the symphony repertoire has been enriched by many eminent composers, including Schubert, Mendelssohn, Schumann, Bruckner, Brahms, Tchaikovsky, Mahler, Sibelius, Elgar, Rachmaninov, Shostakovich and others. The great tradition goes on in an expanding universe of form and meaning. The energies unleashed in the symphony resonate still with freshness and revelation.

## Suggested listening

1732-1809    Haydn, Joseph
             Symphony No.45 in F sharp minor,
             "The Farewell"
             Symphony No.94 in G, "The Surprise"

1756-91      Mozart, Wolfgang Amadeus
             Symphony No.40 in G minor (K550)
             Symphony No. 41 in C (K551), "Jupiter"

1770-1827    Beethoven, Ludwig van
             Symphony No.3 in Eb Op.55, "Eroica"
             Symphony No.5 in C minor Op.67
             Symphony No.6 in F Op.68, "Pastoral"
             Symphony No.7 in A Op.92
             Symphony No.9 in D minor Op.125, "Choral"

1797-1828    Schubert, Franz
             Symphony No.8 in B minor, "The Unfinished"
             Symphony No.9 in C, "The Great"

1809-47      Mendelssohn, Felix
             Symphony No.4 in A Op.90, "Italian"

| | |
|---|---|
| 1833-97 | Brahms, Johannes<br>Symphony No.1 in C minor Op.68 |
| 1840-93 | Tchaikovsky, Peter<br>Symphony No.4 in F minor Op.36<br>Symphony No.6 in B minor Op.74, "Pathétique" |
| 1841-1904 | Dvořák, Antonin<br>Symphony No.9 in E minor Op.95,<br>"From the New World" |
| 1860-1911 | Mahler, Gustav<br>Symphony No.1 in D, "Titan" |
| 1865-1951 | Sibelius, Jean<br>Symphony No.2 in D Op.43 |
| 1891-1953 | Prokofiev, Serge<br>Symphony No.1 in D Op.25, "Classical" |
| 1906-75 | Shostakovich, Dmitri<br>Symphony No.7 Op.60, "Leningrad" |
| 1913-77 | Britten, Benjamin<br>Simple Symphony Op.4 |

# 19

# Concerto

The meeting of the orchestra's symphonic energies and an outstanding instrumentalist is the essence of **concerto**. The soloist, a player of extraordinary ability, blends brilliance and sensitivity with the powers of the orchestra. The results are dazzling displays of musicianship by both parties which have justly made the concerto form exceptionally popular.

Originally the idea of a concerto was less favourable to the soloist. The **concerto grosso** of the late seventeenth and early eighteenth centuries remains distinct from the solo concerto (which developed a little later). The concerto grosso employed two groups of instruments. One group, larger than the other, and known as **ripieno** (or full) provided the main statement of the themes, the smooth flow of bowed sound being punctuated by the rhythmic and harmonic driving force of a harpsichord (referred to as the **continuo**). The second group, the **soli** or **concertino** added contrasting colour and texture.

Among the most famous works in the style of concerto grosso are the Brandenburg Concertos of J.S. Bach, and the concerti grossi of Corelli, Telemann, Handel and Vivaldi are still frequently performed. Vivaldi (c.1675-1741), one of the most prolific composers, was particularly fascinated by the solo concerto. His many compositions of this type for various instruments (such as recorder, flute, oboe, bassoon, trumpet, mandolin, 'cello, not forgetting the four violin concertos known as "The Four Seasons") were a potent influence on Bach — though it is to be noted that Bach was the first composer of concertos for keyboard.

The eighteenth-century composers (as we have seen with the sonata form) possessed dynamic inventive powers. Their development of form was to dominate European composition for the next two hundred years. From now on the creation of sonatas, string quartets, symphonies and concertos would be mandatory for any self-respecting composer. The vocabulary of music with its types of chords, instrumentation and breadth would continue to develop; yet the ways in which composers expressed their ideas remained within the basic schemes formulated by the great composers of the period between 1750 and 1790.

The concerto is a supreme example of this debt to the innovative talents of that classical era. From the time of J.S. Bach, Haydn and Mozart onwards, composers of all nations would endeavour to do justice to the concerto idea. Just as the symphony flowered and flourished, so did the concerto, challenging composers to a display of both musical cooperation and confrontation.

Just as Haydn was the principal initiator of the symphony, so Mozart pioneered the concerto and opened up new possibilities for the composers who followed him. He wrote a great number of works in this form, including not only many keyboard concertos (in which Mozart himself was often the soloist) but also violin concertos (again he could be the soloist), a superb clarinet concerto (a new instrument at the time), four horn concertos, a concerto for flute and harp, and a marvellously inventive **sinfonia concertante** (a concerto with less spectacular display for two or more instruments) for violin and viola.

Composers have often written concertos for themselves to play. Beethoven, Paganini, Chopin, Liszt, Brahms and Rachmaninov are some of the great composer/performers who premièred some or all of their own works. In other instances composers have become fascinated by an instrument they did not play themselves or by a soloist to whose virtuosity they have paid the highest form of tribute in the dedication of a concerto.

Sometimes composers on presenting a concerto to a player have been rebuffed. The performer concerned may have found the work so difficult or so startlingly novel in its approach that it had to be rejected. Leopold Auer, one of the greatest violinists of his day, considered certain passages of Tchaikovsky's Violin Concerto in D (now accepted as an essential part of the repertoire) to be practically unplayable. (Another violinist, Adolf Brodsky, gave the work its première.)

For the composer there are specific problems to be dealt with in the writing of a concerto. Not only is there the question of balance, the need to ensure that the solo instrument is not overwhelmed by the great tidal wave of sound from the orchestra, but also the wider question of interplay between the two contrasting elements must be a major consideration. The orchestra is not just accompanying a soloist, but speaking with a musical voice of its own. What the orchestra has to say must be appropriate to its own medium, and yet totally complementary to the concerto as a whole. The soloist must not steal the centre of the stage without some musical counter-statement from his powerful colleagues.

Since the eighteenth century composers have confronted the challenge of this form. In the process the concerto acquired some of the characteristics of the sonata and symphony shape, but necessarily relinquished others. Concertos, for example, are mostly in three movements, not four. The Minuet and Trio movement was probably discarded in the concerto as this dance form was considered rather inflexible in terms of opportunity for solo display. (An exception to this is Brahms's Piano Concerto No. 2 in Bb where the slow movement is delayed by the second movement in the form of a scherzo and trio.)

As with all music it is content and substance which dominate form. No overall master plan can be fitted to existing concertos that would apply in each case. Yet as with other shapes (such as string quartet or theme and variations) it is worthwhile establishing some guidelines for the inner workings of a concerto.

I

The first movement sets the themes and moods of the work. It introduces the brilliance of the soloist and the textures of his instrument in partnership with the orchestra. This can be done in a number of ways. The most obvious may be to allow the orchestra to open proceedings with a statement of the principal themes. Sometimes this exposition continues for a long while and suspense is built up as the moment approaches when the soloist enters. Once the soloist enters the outlines of melodies so far played can be repeated or the soloist's own voice can be immediately asserted, embellishing available themes or even, in some concertos, launching off into new territory. A feature of the concerto is that we can often expect far more surprises and upheavals in the structural organization than in the symphony. The inclusion of that unpredictable creature — the individual — allows the unexpected to happen.

In the time of Mozart this factor of the unexpected was carried further by the **cadenza**, an improvised passage by the soloist during which the orchestra remains discreetly silent. The cadenza provides an impressive show of instrumental mastery. This became such a popular aspect of the concerto that rather than leave it to the improvisatory abilities of the individual performer, composers, including Mozart, began to add written cadenzas as an integral part of the score.

What the listener can justifiably expect in the first movement of a concerto is the basic scheme of exposition — development — recapitulation. What cannot be predicted are the treatment of themes, the occasions when the soloist will go off at a tangent, and the placing of suitable cadenzas. To suit the needs of various instruments, composers have evolved great flexibility in their methods of writing concertos. In the first movement of the modern work the Concierto de Aranjuez for guitar by Joaquín Rodrigo, the soloist enters first, thereby enabling the small sound of the guitar to be heard distinctly on its own terms before an orchestral passage is pitted against it. (The same device of allowing the soloist to have the first word was used by Beethoven in his Piano Concerto No. 4 in G.)

II
The slow movement of a concerto exploits the innate lyricism of the solo instrument. Here the poetic inspiration of the composer gives the instrument the freedom to make its own way, often reducing the orchestra to a gentle accompanying partner. This combination of soloist and orchestra is frequently marked by a singular beauty.

III
The last movement is generally an energetic spirited finale. After the passionate intensities of the slow movement some release is necessary. The composer may well decide to conclude with a rondo or some other vigorous dance-like form. The concerto ends with virtuosity, vivacity and strength, allowing the soloist and orchestra to reap the harvest of applause and the satisfaction of a brilliant performance.


**Suggested listening**

c. 1675-1741  Vivaldi, Antonio
              Concerti Op.8, "The Four Seasons"

1685-1759     Handel, George Frideric
              Concerti Grossi

1685-1750     Bach, Johann Sebastian
              6 Brandenburg Concertos
              Concerto for 2 Violins and Strings
              in D minor (BWV 1043)

| 1756-91 | Mozart, Wolfgang Amadeus |
|---|---|
| | Concerto for Clarinet and Orchestra in A (K 622) |
| | Concerto for Horn and Strings No.4 in Eb (K 495) |
| | Concerto for Piano and Orchestra No.20 in D minor (K 466) |
| | Concerto for Piano and Orchestra No. 23 in A (K 488) |
| 1770-1827 | Beethoven, Ludwig van |
| | Concerto for Piano and Orchestra No.5 in Eb Op.73, "Emperor" |
| | Concerto for Violin and Orchestra in D Op.61 |
| 1809-47 | Mendelssohn, Felix |
| | Concerto for Violin and Orchestra in E minor Op.64 |
| 1810-49 | Chopin, Frédéric |
| | Concerto for Piano and Orchestra No.1 in E minor Op.11 |
| | Concerto for Piano and Orchestra No. 2 in F minor Op.21 |
| 1810-56 | Schumann, Robert |
| | Concerto for Piano and Orchestra in A minor Op.54 |
| 1811-86 | Liszt, Franz |
| | Concerto for Piano and Orchestra No.1 in Eb |
| 1833-97 | Brahms, Johannes |
| | Concerto for Piano and Orchestra No.1 in D minor Op.15 |
| | Concerto for Piano and Orchestra No.2 in Bb Op.83 |
| | Concerto for Violin and Orchestra in D Op.77 |
| 1838-1920 | Bruch, Max |
| | Concerto for Violin and Orchestra No.1 in G minor Op.26 |
| 1840-93 | Tchaikovsky, Peter |
| | Concerto for Piano and Orchestra No. 1 in Bb minor Op.23 |
| | Concerto for Violin and Orchestra in D Op.35 |

| 1841-1904 | Dvořák, Antonin<br>Concerto for 'Cello and Orchestra<br>in B minor Op.104 |
|-----------|----------------------------------------------------------------------------------|
| 1843-1907 | Grieg, Edvard<br>Concerto for Piano and Orchestra<br>in A minor Op.16 |
| 1857-1934 | Elgar, Edward<br>Concerto for 'Cello and Orchestra<br>in E minor Op.85<br>Concerto for Violin and Orchestra<br>in B minor Op.61 |
| 1837-1943 | Rachmaninov, Sergei<br>Concerto for Piano and Orchestra No.2<br>in C minor Op.18 |
| 1881-1945 | Bartók, Béla<br>Concerto for Orchestra |
| 1902- | Rodrigo, Joaquín<br>Concierto de Aranjuez for Guitar<br>and Orchestra |

# 20

# The Nineteenth Century

The eighteenth century developed the great enduring structures of European music. These forms such as sonata, symphony and concerto are still used by contemporary composers. Yet in the nineteenth century it was inevitable that existing forms should undergo extensive modifications. New structures were also developed, though not all these have continued to attract composers in the twentieth century.

The early nineteenth century witnessed the incoming tide of the great movement known as **romanticism**. Under this influence, literature, the visual arts and music incorporated new techniques and opened up new possibilities, gradually eroding the old values of the classical scheme of things.

**Classicism** could be defined as that which shows a regard for the order, logic and beauty of the classical or ancient world. People imagined that the civilizations of Greece or Rome, at their best, had been founded on principles of logic, reason and balance. Such virtues were admired by the eighteenth century, and its arts, whether architecture, literature, music or painting, tried to interpret the dream of classical perfection.

The classical outlook stressed outward restraint, rational conduct, self-discipline and the qualities of decorum. Romanticism preferred to plumb the depth of the irrational and to explore the dark side of tempestuous feelings. The romantic artist wandered "lonely as a cloud" among the rugged mountains and deep valleys of his own soul. This brooding, isolated aspect of full-blooded romanticism led to an interest in mythology, legend and the cult of past mysterious ages of adventure and the sinister.

To achieve the greatest emotional effect, the romantic composer frequently took pleasure in linking music with a detailed literary scheme or a picturesque descriptive title. Whereas the eighteenth century, on the whole, preferred its music to be absolute, romanticism implied the creation of particular moods. Music requiring an accompanying "programme" of informative notes about the composer's scenario became popular. This approach to composition is known as **programme music**.

The technique of relating music to some external event was not new. Sixteenth century composers such as John Dowland often wrote descriptive works with titles like "Orlando Sleepeth" or "My Lord Willoughby's Welcome Home". Antonio Vivaldi's "Four Seasons" depicts sliding on ice, a drunken stupor, bird song, storms and many other country sounds. Jean Philippe Rameau (1683-1764) wrote harpsichord pieces such as "The Hen", "The Sighs" and "The Whirlwind".

Beethoven's Sonata Op.27, No. 2 was christened the "Moonlight" by a publisher, a name which has endeared this particular sonata to generations of music-lovers. Beethoven himself was not averse to a kind of programme music; the movements of his Sixth Symphony, the "Pastoral", describe particular events, "Awakening of happy feelings on arriving in the country", "By the brook", "Peasants' Merrymaking", "The Storm", "Shepherd's Song; Cheerful and thankful feelings after the storm".

The romantics went even further and made a habit of focusing attention on a title, plot, image or basic mood. This concentration on specific feelings enabled composers to be freer, if they wished, with the formal structure of their work.

The supreme romantic instrument was of course the pianoforte. By the time of Robert Schumann (1810-56), Frédéric Chopin (1810-49) and Franz Liszt (1811-86), the piano had attained its full span of seven octaves (compared with five octaves during Mozart's time) and its expressive resources were greater than ever before.

Schumann's piano works such as *Kinderscenen* ("Scenes from Childhood"), *Carnaval, Waldscenen* ("Forest Scenes"), etc., create many immediate images and portraits. The intimacy of some of these, such as "Dreaming" in "Scenes from Childhood", contrasts with the epic ebullience of the "March against the Philistines" in *Carnaval*. The listener could find the music moving and exciting without knowing the titles, but the intention is best understood by being aware of the topics portrayed.

The piano music of Chopin makes use of varied forms such as nocturnes, scherzos, waltzes, ballades, impromptus, preludes, études and Polish dances like mazurkas and polonaises. Chopin, often described as "the poet of the piano", distrusted the more obvious forms of programme music, but his compositions give an immediate sense of mood and emotion. His application of **rubato** (robbed time — holding back and hurrying on) and new musical forms were indeed innovatory, and his pursuance of chromatic effects (i.e. using notes not part of the main tonality) had a profound effect on musical history. Chopin's strong sense of patriotism for Poland inspired other nationalist composers to seek out the essence of their own country's music. Nationalism became a powerful ingredient in the romantic movement.

Liszt, overwhelmingly impressed by the greatness of Paganini (1782-1840), endeavoured to exploit the resources of the piano in the same way as Paganini had developed the violin: Liszt proved technically and imaginatively well equipped to do so. His piano works often build up gigantic pictures resonating from some central theme, as revealed by titles such as *Les Années de pélerinage* ("The Years of Pilgrimage"), *St François d'Assise prédicant aux oiseaux* ("St Francis of Assisi Preaching to the Birds"), *Etudes d'exécution transcendante* ("Transcendental Studies"), etc.

Schumann, Chopin and Liszt wrote sonatas for the piano, but compared with classical sonata form the listener may be in for some surprises. The romantic concept of sonata is more arbitrary than that of the eighteenth century, though the use and development of themes remains the unifying principle. Such devices as the number of movements or the precise organization of sections veer off, on occasion, from the more predictable classical structures of the sonatas of Haydn, Mozart, Beethoven and Schubert.

Of Chopin's Sonata Op. 35 in B flat minor, Schumann wrote, "The idea of calling it a sonata is a caprice, if not a joke, for he has simply bound together four of his most reckless children." The four movements are actually Agitato (preceded by a slow introduction of four bars), Scherzo, Marche funèbre, and Presto (an unusual and strange last movement, sometimes described as the wind whistling over the gravestones). The third movement, the Funeral March, has become one of the most famous melodies in the world. The romantic sonata has thus provided a slow movement of the greatest expressive power, a monument to the genius of the nineteenth century imagination.

Liszt's only composition in this form, the amazing Sonata in B minor, lasts about half an hour and is in one continuous movement which falls naturally into sections that develop his four main themes. It is a mighty work combining the demonic, the romantic, the religious and the heroic aspects of its brilliant composer. This sonata provides a powerful example of how established musical forms can be subjected to great changes in style and content.

The impact of romanticism on the use of the orchestra can be seen in Hector Berlioz's *Symphonie fantastique*, written three years after Beethoven's death. Programme notes to this symphony are positively essential. The story is of a young musician who poisons himself with opium. In various narcotic dreams he imagines he has killed his beloved and is executed for this crime. The finale, "Witches' Sabbath", is a grisly nightmare in which the image of the beloved joins the horrible hags who attend the musician's funeral.

As well as the scenario, so vital to an appreciation of the symphony, Berlioz makes use of the **idée fixe**, a structural device later exploited to full effect by Richard Wagner in his operas. A small fragment of a tune, a "fixed idea" (or **leitmotiv** as Wagner called it), appears in all five movements of the symphony, suggesting the beloved's presence. Thus a new principle of unity was introduced into the symphonic form, in which the repetition of a specific theme is linked with the portrayal of events in the music itself.

Berlioz (1803-69) steps beyond the framework of the classical symphony by using a wide assortment of instrumental colourings and effects. He not only gives the work a striking title but also adds a subtitle, *Episode de la vie d'un artiste* ("Episode in an artist's life"), and provides a dramatic script. He extends the symphony to five named movements covering specific events — "Dreams and Passions", "A Ball", "In the Fields", "March to the Scaffold" and "The Witches' Sabbath".

His delight in literature extended particularly to Shakespeare and Byron. Berlioz wrote a dramatic symphony, *Romeo and Juliet*, intending here "to write a masterpiece, on a great new plan, a splendid new work, full of passion and imagination . . ." This third symphony of Berlioz involves not only the orchestra but also solo singers and chorus. There are descriptions of the quarrels between Montagues and Capulets, Romeo's love for Juliet, Queen Mab in her chariot, the tomb scene, and a finale of the crowd at the vault, the conflicting families and the reconciliation.

Also inspired by Shakespeare was Felix Mendelssohn (1809-47). His overture to *A Midsummer Night's Dream* was written when he was only seventeen. Later he added other movements including the famous "Wedding March". Another much-loved descriptive work of Mendelssohn's is his Hebrides Overture, also known as "Fingal's Cave". This was written after a visit to Scotland and conjures up images of rock, waves and storm.

A new orchestral form was developed by Liszt, influenced by Berlioz and Mendelssohn. This was the **symphonic poem** or **tone poem**, a single movement structure ideally suited for communicating programmatic images. These symphonic poems by Liszt include "Mazeppa", "Battle of the Huns", "Orpheus" and other colourful stimulants to the imagination. His full-scale symphonies bear the titles *Faust* and *Dante*. *Faust* celebrates Liszt's response to the great drama by Goethe, presenting three massive portraits in music of the principal characters, Faust, Gretchen and Mephistopheles. The work lasts over an hour and makes use of a male voice choir and tenor soloist in the finale.

Romantic elements had been introduced to the art of opera by Carl Maria von Weber (1786-1826). His work, such as *Der Freischütz*, *Euryanthe* and *Oberon*, rejoiced in mysterious fantastic ingredients with magic bullets, medieval castles and the secret world of legend and folk tale. His skilful orchestration brilliantly evoked the atmosphere of drama and myth.

The culmination of romanticism was the work of Richard Wagner (1813-83), a friend of Liszt, and one of the musical giants of the nineteenth century. Wagner's massive use of all the resources of instrumentation, vocal power and dramatic effect of language, integrated with his themes of myth and nationalistic ardour, establish his work as one of the great landmarks of European music. In his operas all the latent trends of the romantic movement find their fulfilment. Not only did he construct a colossal world of the imagination through his operatic representation of the old myths, but his music carries the implications of chromaticism further along the road which was to lead ultimately to the development of atonal music. Wagner's use of a recurring theme, the **leitmotiv** (each associated with various characters, feelings or objects, such as magic swords, love, sleep, fire, Valhalla, the ring, etc.), throughout his operas was both a dramatic device increasing tension and a unifying technique.

Some nineteenth century composers drew back from the imaginative extravagance of romanticism, seeking instead to preserve classical symmetry and clarity. Of these Johannes Brahms (1833-97) is perhaps the foremost. His masters were Bach and Beethoven and his sonatas, symphonies and concertos are far from the concepts of programme music.

Brahms was particularly fond of the variation form and wrote several sets of these. In his Variations and Fugue on a Theme of Handel Op. 24 for piano there are twenty-five variations culminating in a titanic fugue. The St Anthony Variations and the last movement of the Fourth Symphony are brilliant examples of his orchestral writing in this form. Brahms' penchant for variations is an indication of continuity between classicism and the mid-nineteenth century.

In Brahms' piano music we find the forms of **capriccio, rhapsody** and **intermezzo**. (Liszt wrote over a dozen Hungarian Rhapsodies.) These fairly vague musical terms leave the composer enough freedom to invest the form with his own meaning.

The Hungarian Dances of Brahms, written for piano duet, stimulated other composers such as Dvořák and Grieg to write dances with strong national characteristics. The influence of nationalism in music became one of the most potent forces, adding new colours to the palette of European culture.

Nowadays the immensely popular compositions of Tchaikovsky (1840-93) could be regarded as some of the most vividly nationalist music of the nineteenth century. The passionate outpouring of his symphonies and concertos, the searing intensity of his orchestration, and the brooding introversion of his powerful melodies, are now recognized as the finest product of Russian romanticism. Yet his wide admiration of classical forms caused him to be regarded by other Russian composers of his time as more "westernized" than they were. His music has transcended these definitions, and while remaining Russian to the core, has proved of perennial appeal to all nations.

Meanwhile the Russian identity of Borodin (1833-87), Mussorgsky (1839-81), and Rimsky-Korsakov (1844-1908), the Czech symphonic poem *Má Vlast* ("My Fatherland") by Smetena (1824-84), and the Bohemian flavour of much of the music of Dvořák (1841-1904), the Norwegian voice of Grieg (1843-1907), and the Spanish evocations of Albeniz (1860-1909) are some of the manifestations of specific national style which emerged. Such music brought together the spectacular vision of individual composers with an assertion of the indigenous musical qualities of nations.

The musical forms through which this sense of national identity revealed itself are many and varied. They range from the operas of Verdi (1813-1901), who was a powerful force in the political unification of Italy, to the Peer Gynt Suites by Grieg and the geographical pictorialism of Albeniz's pianoforte music. It was

the coming together of so many musical developments throughout the entire nineteenth century which made such diversity
possible.

## Suggested listening

1792-1868    Rossini, Gioacchino
Overture, "The Barber of Seville"
Overture, "The Thieving Magpie"
Overture, "William Tell"

1803-69    Berlioz, Hector
Overture, *Le Carnaval Romain*
Overture, *Le Corsaire*
Overture, *Les Francs juges*
*Symphonie fantastique*

1809-47    Mendelssohn, Felix
Overture, "The Hebrides" ("Fingal's Cave")
A Midsummer Night's Dream (Incidental Music)

1810-49    Chopin, Frédéric
Nocturne No.2 in Eb Op.9
Polonaise in A Op.40, "Military"
Sonata No.2 in Bb minor Op.35
Waltz No.1 in Eb Op.18

1810-56    Schumann, Robert
Carnaval Op.9
Kinderscenen Op.15
Song Cycle — *Dichterliebe* Op.48

1811-86    Liszt, Franz
*Faust* Symphony
Hungarian Rhapsodies
*Liebesträume*

1813-83    Wagner, Richard
Overture, "The Flying Dutchman"
Overture, "The Mastersingers"
Overture, *Tannhäuser*
Liebestod from *Tristan und Isolde*
"Ride of the Valkyries" from *Die Walküre*

| 1824-84 | Smetena, Bedrich<br>Symphonic Poems, *Má Vlast* |
|---|---|
| 1833-87 | Borodin, Alexander<br>Polovtsian Dances from *Prince Igor* |
| 1833-97 | Brahms, Johannes<br>Academic Festival Overture<br>Hungarian Dances<br>Tragic Overture |
| 1835-1921 | Saint-Saëns, Camille<br>*Danse macabre* Op.40 |
| 1838-75 | Bizet, Georges<br>Suites, *L'Arlésienne*<br>Suites, *Carmen* |
| 1839-81 | Mussorgsky, Modeste<br>Night on the Bare Mountain<br>Pictures from an Exhibition |
| 1840-93 | Tchaikovsky, Peter<br>Ballet music: *The Nutcracker*<br>*The Sleeping Beauty*<br>*Swan Lake*<br>1812 Overture<br>Fantasy Overture, "Romeo and Juliet" |
| 1843-1907 | Grieg, Edvard<br>Peer Gynt Suites |
| 1844-1908 | Rimsky-Korsakov, Nikolas<br>Symphonic Suite, "Scheherazade" |
| 1865-1957 | Sibelius, Jean<br>Finlandia Op.26<br>Karelia Suite Op.11<br>Legend Op.22 "The Swan of Tuonela"<br>En Saga Op.9<br>Symphonic Poem Op.112, "Tapiola"<br>Valse triste |

# 21

# Twentieth - Century Music

The twentieth century already possesses an exciting musical history. Never before has so much music been so easily available. The invention of the gramophone and the massive developments of radio and television have made music accessible during everyday life to an unprecedented degree. The age-old dreams of humanity, to fly, to travel quickly and to preserve records of living sound, have been triumphantly realized. Sometimes such dreams have turned to nightmare; the means of travelling, the reproduction of music in public places, and various other technological marvels, produce a cage of noise within which we are trapped for life.

The impact of history and technological progress on music during this century has been crucial. The dislocation and chaos of two world wars, the instability of world peace and the high-speed pace of modern life are inevitably reflected in contemporary art. Modern music recreates the hectic rhythms and the sense of disturbance felt by people of many nations.

Music is often blamed for portraying the harsher realities of modern living. One might as well blame a mirror for reflecting the care-worn lines of a tired face. Though a purpose of music might often be to soothe and distract, the composer must also be honest about the world we inhabit. The message of modern music is ominous and threatening; but the reality of the twentieth century, with its unspeakable horrors of the past and profound uncertainties of the future, is far more menacing than music can ever express. Though many individuals may act like ostriches, burying their heads in the sand by ignoring the stark facts of twentieth-century existence, the onslaught of the contemporary world on the imagination cannot be disregarded.

Certainly in the twentieth century much of the popular music disseminated daily through radio and television could be seen as musical tranquillizers meant for mass consumption and intended to lull, bemuse and soothe. The use of sugary massed violins as background music in airports and supermarkets, the nostalgic melodiousness of daily music of earlier decades — all are bromides designed to induce a feeling of well-being, sophistication and poise. The smooth musical wallpaper of the cocktail pianist, the elegant saxophones of the formal ballroom and the unobtrusive meanderings of a Palm Court orchestra were similar manifestations of a particularly twentieth century product.

Nowadays, because of the cost of hiring musicians, the blandness of background music in hotels, bars and restaurants is taken one stage further by infiltrating music on an endlessly revolving tape to provide an inexpensive aural backcloth. In previous centuries music could never be heard without musicians being present. The twentieth century phenomenon has been to disembody music, giving us background sound but with no necessity to respond to it by way of applause or acknowledgement.

First jazz and then rock music have fought hard and well against the polite concept of music as mere ornamental background. Jazz singers traditionally transcended the well-disciplined rhythms of formal dance music and the trite sentiments of popular ballads. Improvisation and spontaneity cut through the subservient role expected of musicians. The style of "bebop" cut loose even further, forcing modernistic harmonies and angular cross-rhythms into the language of jazz.

Rock music developed in rebellion and dissent against the smooth nothingness of so much popular music of the fifties. The short-haired, bow-tied, dinner-jacketed image of the dance band musician was replaced by the long-haired, agitated youthfulness of the pop musician attired either in outrageously colourful clothes or casual denims.

Rock music has evolved its own vocabulary and succeeded in finding a way of communicating to millions of people. From unpretentious beginnings it has now come to be taken seriously as a medium of expression. Constantly renewing its vitality, the horizons of rock (with its musical structures founded on one or more vocalists, guitar, keyboard electric bass guitar and many other instruments, all moulded together by the pounding pulse of the drummer) have expanded till differing nations have united in listening to what it has to say.

In the meantime composers outside the embrace of "popular" music have retreated more and more into their private world. The twentieth century found it necessary quite early on to make great adjustments to the principles of musical creation which had dominated previous centuries. In particular "serious" composers urgently desired to forge a new musical language capable of expressing the new world which thrust itself in upon them.

In the visual arts, in literature and drama, intense experimentation also took place. The novels of James Joyce, the poetry of T.S.Eliot and the paintings of Picasso, are three significant examples of profound upheavals in the textures and structures of European art. Though later these artists were accepted as part of the establishment, their early cataclysmic struggles led to much opposition from the old guard.

The musical revolutionaries who created and refined a whole new language for themselves were Arnold Schoenberg (1874-1951) and his pupils/disciples, Anton von Webern (1883-1945) and Alban Berg (1885-1935). The core of their efforts was centred on the establishment of the **twelve note** system. To many people the work of these three is still difficult and even unacceptable, but others, and particularly composers, have discovered new guidelines within their work which are of great value in the development of a new musical language.

Schoenberg believed that the traditional concepts of tonality (see Chapter 4) had become exhausted and could no longer produce anything except imitations and feeble attempts to recreate past glories. The idea that music must be in a particular key had been breaking down in one way or another since the time of Beethoven. The freedom of tonality displayed by Chopin and Wagner and the extensive use of chromaticism in the nineteenth century, seemed to demand a new theoretical and practical approach to composition.

The work of Claude Debussy (1862-1918) represents another milestone on the road to the disintegration of the European tonal system. Influenced by painters and poets, Debussy brought the movement of Impressionism into music. In his compositions Debussy sought to give a vivid "impression" of pictorial images. His titles such as *La Mer* ("The Sea"), *Prélude à l'après-midi d'un faune* ("Prelude to the afternoon of a faun"), *La Fille aux cheveux de lin* ("The girl with the flaxen hair"), *La Cathédrale engloutie* ("The submerged cathedral"), *Des pas sur la neige* ("Footsteps in the snow"), *Clair de lune* ("Moonlight"), *Feux d'artifice* ("Fireworks"), *Reflets dans l'eau* ("Reflections in the water"), etc. all indicate the evocative nature of his music.

By skilfully integrating effects such as the use of the old church modes, the whole tone scale (dividing the octave into six steps instead of seven), parallel movement of intervals, the oriental flavour of the pentatonic scale and dissonant chords which did not resolve into the usual cadences coming home to the tonic key, Debussy rejected conventional ideas of tonality and propelled the art of music into the twentieth century. He became a major influence on subsequent composers and also much appreciated by the general public: his *Clair de lune*, for example, has become as much a favourite as Beethoven's "Moonlight" Sonata.

If Debussy directed music towards new tonal horizons, it was Schoenberg who took the process even further. Composers, as has been mentioned, had been edging towards a chromatic freedom which verged on the **atonal** (i.e. music with little or no feeling of a central key). In particular Wagner's *Tristan und Isolde* (premièred in 1865) represents one of the keenest precedents of atonal elements, whilst the music of Gustav Mahler (1860-1911), Alexander Scriabin (1872-1915) and Richard Strauss (1864-1949) bears dramatic witness to the loosening of the fabric of tonality.

Composers seemed intent on finding a way of avoiding the necessity of writing music in specific keys. But breaking away from tonality was as difficult as a rocket's attempt to defy the earth's gravitational pull with underpowered engines. It was Schoenberg who finally went into orbit and discovered the secrets of writing atonal music. This was to affect the whole strategy of composition, altering the basis of melody, home keys and the resolution of chords.

Why did Arnold Schoenberg find it necessary to do this? Why was it not possible for composers to go on writing according to European tonality? The second question is perhaps easier to answer than the first. Some composers after all did indeed go on writing in traditional styles. But the music of those who preferred conventional tonality is now regarded as belonging to the old world and not to the new. Out of the shadow of nineteenth-century art forms, the twentieth century vision was waiting to be born. Composers could cling to the old patterns and techniques or attempt to come to terms with a different world. The new, however, could only emerge through experiment, bold new ideas, struggle and anguish.

Schoenberg's solution to the problems of atonal music was not, of course, the complete answer. But his efforts enabled composers to grasp more clearly the nature of the crisis. Other great musical thinkers, such as Bartók, would suggest alternative ways to tackle the issue. What was clear however was that Schoenberg's ideas and innovations could not be ignored. Composers were coming to the conclusion that the old basis of composition was no longer sufficient or satisfactory. Atonal aspects in music were now so widespread and yet so misunderstood that it became essential for someone to investigate and systematize the new musical vocabulary.

By the time he was ready to jettison the idea of writing music in specific keys, Schoenberg had already traversed other phases of development. These included earlier traditional works as well as experiments in free atonality. In the 1920s he unleashed on the world his new method of using the twelve semitones of the **chromatic scale** as the basic unit of composition. Each of the twelve notes was to be considered as equal to each of its companions; the discipline of the tonic note was now to be challenged.

The chromatic scale's twelve notes are as follows:

                                                  B

                                         A sharp

                                    A

                               G sharp

                            G

                        F sharp

                    F

                E

            D sharp

        D

      C sharp

C

Schoenberg's compositional method was first to put these twelve notes in a particular order, chosen by the composer. Of the available permutations for twelve notes (without repetition) there are 479,001,600 possibilities, so a composer has plenty to choose from. When the twelve semitones have been placed in the chosen order, the result is the *Tonreihe* or **note row**. The note row is often written out above a composition of this kind.

In Schoenberg's method of twelve note composition, the notes follow each other throughout the work in the precise order established by the note row. This is known as **serialism**. In works derived from the note row, the individual notes themselves can be of any length, at any octave; the row can be played forwards, backwards, inverted, or transposed. But the order of the sequence is to be kept throughout.

Schoenberg's immediate followers, Berg and Webern, hammered out new shapes and structures within which to deploy this startling development. Webern's music uses the twelve note system with sparseness and economy. His Six Bagatelles (1913) for string quartet, for example, lasts no longer than three and a half minutes. Webern's entire output is contained within approximately four hours' listening time. Yet he has proved a most influential advocate of the twelve note method.

Alban Berg found fame with his opera *Wozzeck*, a freely atonal work with occasional tonal elements. His Violin Concerto, dedicated to the memory of a young actress who died at the age of eighteen, is a remarkable fusion of a traditional form with the twelve note system. His other opera *Lulu* has proved in recent years to be a powerful dramatic success.

In one way or another most leading composers of the twentieth century have needed to confront the forces of atonality. This does not mean that they all had to tread a Schoenbergian path towards serialism.

Béla Bartók (1881-1945) is an example of a composer who found artistic salvation in quite a different way. He developed an original musical language of his own, incorporating the exotic scales and vigorous rhythms of Hungarian and Rumanian folk music. At the same time as he absorbed and transmuted the rich material of folk cultures, he made use of the classical forms of European music, such as the string quartet and concerto.

Igor Stravinsky (1882-1971) met almost every aspect of twentieth-century musical development head on. The breadth of his output spans the range of stylistic and technical innovations of the changing decades. In this respect Stravinsky's prolific artistry is comparable with Picasso; these two great figures towered over their respective territories and established a unique dominance.

The sixty years of Stravinsky's musical creativity include ballets such as *The Firebird* (1910), *Petrushka* (1911) and *The Rite of Spring* (1913), operas such as *Oedipus Rex* (1927) and *The Rake's Progress* (1951) and many songs, symphonies, concertos and chamber works.

Stravinsky's music with its violent rhythms and spectacular orchestration burst on the public like a hurricane. The première of *The Rite of Spring* caused an uproar of protest in the theatre. A few years after this Stravinsky turned to **neo-classicism**, a movement which sought the inner spirit and meaning of eighteenth-century ideals, particularly in respect of clarity of texture and formal balance. This was a reaction to the lush extravagances of late romanticism. Later in his life Stravinsky fell under the spell of serialism, inspired by the example of Webern.

Born thirteen years after Stravinsky, Paul Hindemith (1895-1963), was also drawn to neo-classicism. He wished to lessen the misunderstanding which sometimes separated composer from audience so began to write works designed to be played by amateur musicians; this was known as **Gebrauchsmusik** ("music for use"). He was concerned not only with composition but also with teaching and expounding his musical ideas. His book, *The Craft of Musical Composition*, sets out his beliefs and theories on reconciling traditional tonality with contemporary trends.

Hindemith's music was banned in Nazi Germany (as was that of Schoenberg, Berg and Webern) which caused him to leave Germany and settle for a while in the United States, returning to Europe after the war. Totalitarian regimes react strongly against many aspects of experimentation in music, literature and the visual arts. In Russia composers such as Serge Prokofiev (1891-1953) and Dmitri Shostakovich (1906-75) felt the heavy pressure of censorship on frequent occasions. How these composers would have developed if left entirely to their own devices is naturally impossible to estimate. As it happened both continued the traditions of symphony, ballet and opera, as well as many chamber and instrumental works.

In Britain the major figures of twentieth century music include Edward Elgar (1857-1934), Frederick Delius (1862-1934), Ralph Vaughan Williams (1872-1958), William Walton (1902-  ), Lennox Berkeley (1903-  ), Michael Tippett (1905-  ) and Benjamin Britten (1913-77). Elgar is the epitome of the late Romantic preferring to shape a characteristically English art from traditional forms and vocabulary. His oratorios, concertos, symphonies and other orchestral works look back nostalgically to the age of a secure tonality. Delius could be called the English Impressionist with his beautiful and poetic evocations of nature in his orchestral and operatic works. Vaughan Williams, like

Bartók, became one of the great researchers of folk song, incorporating the energies of its melodies and rhythms into his own musical idiom.

Benjamin Britten dominated the post-war years of British music. His many operas and large-scale choral works (including the War Requiem composed in 1962) as well as a wide range of orchestral and solo works achieved international acclaim. His love of the voice, demonstrated in many choral works including nearly a dozen operas, makes his work human and approachable. His musical language has been absorbed into the blood stream of all British composers. Yet at no time did Britten ever move into the realm of the aggressively avant-garde or into territory where his audience would be reluctant to follow.

The United States has produced a remarkable compendium of twentieth-century sound. The glittering history of jazz and popular entertainment has undoubtedly been America's greatest musical gift to the world. At the same time American composers such as George Gershwin (1898-1937) and Aaron Copland (1900-    ) have attempted to assimilate jazz influence within their work. Gershwin's Rhapsody in Blue (premièred in 1924) is perhaps the best example of a fusion between jazz and "serious" styles. Copland went on to delve more into the folk aspects of American music and later explored serialism.

American composers frequently studied in Europe; they were also affected by the presence of distinguished European musicians, such as Schoenberg, Stravinsky, Milhaud (1892-1974), Castelnuovo-Tedesco (1895-1968), and others who settled or resided for some years in the USA. In return, European composers, including Stravinsky, exerted strenuous efforts to bring jazz elements into their music.

Since the end of World War II, composers such as Olivier Messiaen (1908-    ), John Cage (1912-    ), Luciano Berio (1925-    ), Pierre Boulez (1925-    ) and Karlheinz Stockhausen (1928-    ) have attempted to move music even further from the aura of nineteenth century Romanticism. The post-1945 period saw a massive increase in experimentation of many kinds. The traditional elements of rhythm, melody, harmony, form, instrumentation and texture have been expanded to include sounds and noises not considered part of music by previous generations.

The use of electronic sound, new instrumental techniques (such as playing *inside* the piano directly on the strings), unprecedented vocal effects (including whispering, repetition of words, sighing, etc.), a wide spectrum of percussive devices, dramatic elongated silences, the discarding of conventional formal structures, and the introduction of **aleatoric music** (from the Latin word for "dice", music which contains an element of chance so that each time it is played the result could be different), have created a new world of musical experience.

In retrospect the twentieth century offers a tangled web of immense complexity. The shape of its music is as diverse and confused as the pattern of its historical events. Composers have continued to write good music despite the dislocation of war, social upheaval, exile, tyranny and the sense of deep moral insecurity which have characterized these troubled years.

The movements of nationalism, late Romanticism, neo-classicism, jazz, serialism, free atonality and post-Webern grappling with adventurous experiments in sound have succeeded in bringing forth many notable works. Time alone will evaluate their ultimate worth. In the meantime, as with previous centuries, musical structures, language and theory, continue to challenge our prejudices and assumptions. Composers of many nations work to ensure that the life-affirming essence of music does not diminish.

## Suggested listening

1857-1934    Elgar, Edward
Chanson de Matin
Introduction and Allegro for Strings
Pomp and Circumstance Marches

1862-1918    Debussy, Claude
*La Cathédrale engloutie*
(Piano prelude No.10, Book 1)
*Clair de lune*
*La Fille aux cheveux de lin*
(Piano prelude No.8, Book 1)
*La Mer*
*Nocturnes*
*Prélude à l'après-midi d'un faune*

1862-1934    Delius, Frederick
On hearing the first cuckoo in spring
The Walk to the Paradise Garden
(from *A Village Romeo and Juliet*)

| 1864-1949 | Strauss, Richard |
| | *Also sprach Zarathustra* — Symphonic Poem |
| | *Don Juan* — Symphonic Poem |
| | *Till Eulenspiegel* — Symphonic Poem |

1864-1949     Strauss, Richard
*Also sprach Zarathustra* — Symphonic Poem
*Don Juan* — Symphonic Poem
*Till Eulenspiegel* — Symphonic Poem

1872-1958     Vaughan Williams, Ralph
Fantasia on Greensleeves
Fantasia on a Theme by Thomas Tallis

1874-1934     Holst, Gustav
The Planets

1874-1951     Schoenberg, Arnold
*Pierrot Lunaire* Op.21
*Varklärte Nacht* ("Transfigured Night") Op.4

1875-1937     Ravel, Maurice
Bolero
Daphnis and Chloe
Mother Goose Suite
*Pavane pour une Infante défunte*

1876-1946     Falla, Manuel de
Ritual Fire Dance from *El Amor Brujo*
         ("Love the Magician")
The Three-Cornered Hat

1881-1945     Bartók, Béla
Mikrocosmos
The Miraculous Mandarin
Rumanian Folkdances
String Quartets 1-6

1882-1967     Kodály, Zoltán
Dances of Galánta
Dances of Marosszék
Suite "Háry János"

1882-1971     Stravinsky, Igor
*The Firebird*
*Petrushka*
*The Rite of Spring*

1883-1945     Webern, Anton
6 Bagatelles for String Quartet Op.9
Symphony Op.21

| 1885-1935 | Berg, Alban |
| | *Lulu* (opera) |
| | *Wozzeck* (opera) |
| | Concerto for Violin and Orchestra |

| 1891-1953 | Prokofiev, Serge |
| | Peter and the Wolf |
| | Romeo and Juliet |

| 1895-1963 | Hindemith, Paul |
| | *Mathis der Maler* |

| 1898-1937 | Gershwin, George |
| | An American in Paris |
| | Porgy and Bess |
| | Rhapsody in Blue |

| 1900-50 | Weill, Kurt |
| | *Rise and Fall of the City of Mahogonny* |
| | *The Threepenny Opera* |

| 1900- | Copland, Aaron |
| | Appalachian Spring |
| | Billy the Kid |
| | Rodeo |
| | El Salon Mexico |

| 1902- | Walton, William |
| | Belshazzar's Feast |
| | Concerto for Violà and Orchestra |
| | Coronation March — Crown Imperial |
| | Façade |

| 1903-78 | Khachaturian, Aram |
| | Gayaneh |
| | Masquerade |
| | Spartacus |

| 1903- | Berkeley, Lennox |
| | Serenade for Strings Op.12 |

| 1905- | Tippett, Michael |
| | A Child of Our Time |
| | *The Midsummer Marriage* (opera) |

| 1908- | Messiaen, Olivier |
| | Vingt regards sur l'Enfant Jesus |

| 1910-81 | Barber, Samuel<br>Adagio for Strings |
| 1913-77 | Britten, Benjamin<br>Sea Interludes from *Peter Grimes* |
| 1925- | Boulez, Pierre<br>*Le Marteau sans maître*<br>*Pli selon pli* |
| 1928- | Stockhausen, Karlheinz<br>*Kontakte* |
| 1931- | Williamson, Malcolm<br>Our Man in Havana |

## Suggested further reading

Abraham, Gerald, *Design in Music*, Oxford, Oxford University Press, 1949.

Alberti, Luciano, *Music through the Ages,* London, Cassell, 1974.

Bernstein, Leonard, *The Joy of Music,* London, White Lion Press, 1971 and Simon & Schuster, New York.

Blackwood, Alan, *The Pageant of Music*, London, Barrie & Jenkins, 1977.

Copland, Aaron, *Music and Imagination*, Harvard, Mass., Harvard University Press, new edition 1972.

Copland, Aaron, *What to Listen for in Music,* New York, McGraw-Hill/Mentor, 1957.

Daniels, Robin, *Conversations with Menuhin,* London, MacDonald Futura, 1980 and St Martin's Press, New York.

Deri, Otto, *Exploring Twentieth Century Music,* New York, Holt, Rinehart & Winston, 1968.

Gammond, Peter, *The Meaning and Magic of Music,* London, Hamlyn, 1968.

Griffiths, Paul, *A Concise History of Modern Music*, London, Thames & Hudson, 1978.

Headington, Christopher, *The Bodley Head History of Western Music,* London, Bodley Head, 1977 and Schirmer Books, New York.

Hindemith, Paul, *A Composer's World*, Harvard, Mass., Harvard University Press, 1952.

Holst, Imogen, *An ABC of Music*, Oxford, Oxford University Press, 1963.

Hopkins, Anthony, *Talking about Music*, London, Heinemann Educational Books, 1977.

Hopkins, Anthony, *Understanding Music*, London, J.M. Dent, 1977.

Hurd, Michael, *The Composer*, Oxford, Oxford University Press, 1968.

Károlyi, Ottó, *Introducing Music*, Harmondsworth, Penguin, 1965.

Lang, Paul and Bettman, Otto, *A Pictorial History of Music*, New York, Norton, 1960.

Morris, R.O., *The Structure of Music*, Oxford, Oxford University Press, 1935.

Percival, Allen, *History of Music*, Teach Yourself Series, London, English Universities Press, 1961.

Routh, Francis, *Contemporary Music*, Teach Yourself Series, London, English Universities Press, 1968.

Scholes, Percy A., *The Listener's Guide to Music*, Oxford, Oxford University Press, 1961.

Smith Brindle, Reginald, *The New Music*, Oxford, Oxford University Press, 1975.

Stevenson, Ronald, *Western Music — An Introduction*, London, Kahn & Averill, 1971.

# Index

Also available from Allison & Busby

Leonard Williams
**THE DANCING CHIMPANZEE**
A study of the origins of primitive music

In this book Leonard Williams writes about two subjects which
hold a lifelong interest for him: music and animal behaviour. His
purpose is to disprove the thesis that the music of primitive man
is a development of the cries and drumming actions of the apes, a
thesis which has been too generally accepted since it was first
postulated by Darwin.

Williams argues that this theory results from a deep misappre-
hension of the nature of music, which is essentially rhythmic
rather than melodic. Having spent many years studying the
behaviour of apes, Leonard Williams is also a confirmed
unbeliever in their aesthetic abilities; he argues that art in
general, and music in particular, arises out of a sense of self-
consciousness, a recognition of individual existence, a fear of the
external world and a desire to penetrate and placate its mysteries,
all of which are essentially human functions.

As a distinguished jazz and classical musician (father and teacher
of the guitarist John Williams) Leonard Williams worked for
many years with the Australian Broadcasting Commission and
was the founder of the Spanish Guitar Centre in London. He
now lives with his family and a colony of woolly monkeys at the
Monkey Sanctuary near Looe in Cornwall.

"Fascinating" — Yehudi Menuhin

"Leonard Williams combines what must be the unique qualifi-
cations of musician and monkey-minder. In this concise, expert
analysis he scouts the idea that music exists in nature"
— Kenneth Allsop, *Evening Standard*

"Thanks to the Leonard Williamses of this world, animal
behaviourists are at last beginning to recognize and reconnoitre
the controversial realm of animal aesthetics" — Malcolm Troup,
*Head of Music, The City University*

5876